KT-477-296

love your

Paul Mendelson is the London *Financial Times* bridge correspondent, and a leading author on bridge, poker and casino gambling.

Paul switched from chess to bridge while still at school, and has stayed with the game. Although competitive, he only rarely plays tournament bridge these days, but he can claim the National Schools' Championship (a while back now), representing England in the European Friendly Games in 1984, two gold and two silver medals in several Mind Sports Olympiads and the Scottish National Championships – pairs and teams trophies, as well as numerous county and regional events.

Paul is the author of seven books on bridge, three books on poker, and a huge book on the statistically correct way to play every casino game. He writes the *Financial Times'* bridge column weekly and his articles appear in magazines throughout the world. For many years the administrator of the Macallan International Pairs Championship, Paul is known to many of the world's finest players and is constantly seeking high-level innovations for his teaching and play.

His interactive lectures are renowned, allowing players of all standards to improve their game. Never relying on rules, he insists on explaining the logical thought processes behind each decision. His students have gone on to win many competitions, and he has coached expert players, training them for international competition.

9510000182451

Other titles

Bridge for Complete Beginners
Control the Bidding
The Right Way to Play Bridge
Bridge: Winning Ways to Play Your Cards
Texas Hold'em Poker: Begin and Win
Texas Hold'em Poker: Win Online
The Mammoth Book of Poker
The Mammoth Book of Casino Games
The Golden Rules of Bridge

Thinking About Bridge

A thought-based approach to declarer play, defence and bidding judgement

Paul Mendelson

ROBINSON

ROBINSON

First published in Great Britain in
2018 by Robinson

Copyright © Paul Mendelson, 2018

10 9 8 7 6 5 4 3 2 1

The moral right of the author has
been asserted.

All rights reserved.
No part of this publication may be
reproduced, stored in a retrieval
system, or transmitted, in any form,
or by any means, without the prior
permission in writing of the
publisher, nor be otherwise
circulated in any form of binding or
cover other than that in which it is
published and without a similar
condition including this condition
being imposed on the subsequent
purchaser.

A CIP catalogue record for this book
is available from the British Library

ISBN: 978-1-47214-185-9

Typeset in Sentinel and Scala Sans
by Mousemat Design Limited

Printed and bound in Great Britain by
CPI Group (UK) Ltd, Croydon CR0 4YY

Papers used by Robinson are from
well-managed forests and other
responsible sources

Robinson
An imprint of
Little, Brown Book Group
Carmelite House
50 Victoria Embankment
London EC4Y 0DZ

An Hachette UK Company
www.hachette.co.uk

www.littlebrown.co.uk

Contents

3 BIDDING CONCEPTS

Abbreviations

4C*	An asterisk after a bid indicates a conventional (non-natural) bid, which will have been or is about to be explained in the text.
GSF	Grand Slam Force
LHO	Left-hand opponent
LTC	Losing Trick Count
RHO	Right-hand opponent
4SF	Fourth Suit Forcing – the essential convention – see *Control the Bidding*
UCB	Unassuming Cue-bid
UNT	Unusual No-Trump
Blackwood	Is used to indicate any form of Blackwood you prefer
RKCB	Roman Key-Card Blackwood – my preference.
TTP	Total Trumps Principle
4H	A number and capital letter indicates a bid or contract
3♣ / ♦AKQ	A suit symbol and number/letters indicate card(s)
Balanced-ish	This refers to a hand which, if one card were to be moved to somewhere else, the hand would be balanced. For example:

♠ AKJ2

♥ K7

♦ AQ

♣ KJ1074

This is a balanced-ish hand because, if 4♣ were a heart or a diamond, the hand would, indeed, be balanced. As it is, this hand is quite suitable for a 2NT opener, showing a balanced hand.

Never	Almost never
Always	Almost always

Introduction

When you start playing bridge, there is so much to learn, to absorb, to remember, that most of your brain is being used to retain this information, recalling what each bid means in context, your basic leads, signals and discards, and the standard declarer plays required for success.

This book is for players who have a decent grasp of the basics, and seek to spend more time *thinking* about bridge, rather than trying to remember what they have been taught. And this is how you improve at bridge, whether you are in your second or third year of playing, or whether you've been working on your game for decades: as material becomes second nature to you, there is space in your brain to consider more exciting things.

The book is in three sections. When it comes to card play, you want to try to form a picture of your opponents' hand(s), and this can be achieved through attention to the auction, your partnership's agreement on leads, signals and discards, and new ways to think about problems. These methods are not based on a formula, on remembering rules, or consulting flow charts – this is thinking through the hand for yourself to reach interesting, exciting and ultimately empowering (in bridge terms) conclusions.

The first section on Declarer Play will introduce you to, or remind you of, ways of thinking that will help you to develop successful Avoidance plays; create key Endplays and Squeezes to bring home contracts which would otherwise have failed; to manufacture alternative Finesse positions, and entries to a key hand; to interpret and read your opponents' cards and what they reveal about their hands. At a higher level yet, you must be practised in occluding from your opponents the vital information they will be seeking in order to find a way to defeat you.

In the section on Defence, I'll try to help you and your partner to lead more successfully, signal and discard to provide clear and crucial information, interpret and anticipate the declarer's plan and hence have a better chance to thwart it.

To succeed, we will look at unconventional NT leads and trick counting in defence – both your own side's and declarer's, learn about Surround plays, Entry-killing plays, and judge when to use your own or partner's entries. In doing so, you will improve your capacity and create time to consider not only which suit to play, but which card. Tricks will be changed beyond recognition, as you limit what your opponents are able to do, withhold information from them, and maintain control of the hand.

What I love about card play is that the play and defence are intimately linked – the better you get at one discipline, the more potential you have to improve the other. This is because in order to form the best play, you must interpret what your opponent is doing and strive to counter their actions directly. And this is true when it comes to your opposition too. Instead of trying to avoid the best pair at your club, make a bee-line for them. You always want to play with and against the best players you can find, because this is the most effective way to improve your game. You may get criticised – hopefully in a constructive friendly way – but, if the criticism is justified, that knowledge will help you to improve.

The last section, on Bidding, looks at how you might supplement a modern Acol-style bidding system with some useful gadgets and partnership understandings. If you play a system closer to Standard American, there will be plenty of ideas you can adapt and adopt to suit you too. Just as importantly, I suggest that there are some gadgets which aren't such a good idea to play. Above all, you want your bidding to help you to judge the right contract – be it making or as a sacrifice – to inform your partner without giving away too much about your hand to your opponents, and constantly to challenge your opposition to make tough decisions.

As so many of my students now enjoy playing Duplicate Pairs, I have included a Convention Card with suggestions as to the best Acol-based system you might play. Players who have looked at one of my previous books, *Control the Bidding*, can add the innovations included in this book to their previous knowledge, eliminate the illogical elements of their system, and include only the most powerful and useful elements. A streamlined, logical system, without too much complication, will definitely serve you best in the long run.

I always tell my students that bridge is a thinking woman's game.

People who play just to socialise, push cards around the table and tell one another off, will hopefully enjoy their game – it is a great social asset – but bridge becomes a more and more satisfying game the better you get at it. The techniques in this book will not only improve your score but, once you and your partner (or group of bridge friends) become familiar with them, will increase your enjoyment too, as you begin to see just how amazingly brilliant this game of ours is.

It's time for a pronoun change in this tome. Previously, mainly for ink-saving purposes, I usually referred to players as 'he'. This time, it will be 'she'. Most of my students are women and, since many hands in this book are taken from my classes, it is only right that those guileful, thoughtful and ingenious members of the opposite sex are given full credit where it's due.

Paul Mendelson
London

1
DECLARER PLAY

What to Think About as Declarer

Assume that leads against NT contracts are from a five-card suit

Let's start this section with something very simple but which gets you off to a really good start.

When you play in a NT contract and your opponent leads, assume that it is from a five-card suit.

If you follow the Rule of 7, or the Rule of 11, or the Rule of David Beckham, that's great. The problem is that you are following a rule and not thinking – and *thinking* about bridge is what you must do if you are going to succeed. So, ditch the rule, and assume that the leader has got a five-card suit. If she only has four cards, you are likely to succeed anyway; if she has a six-card suit, assuming five cards will cover this longer holding anyway. Best of all, if you take a moment to count out the opponent's suit at trick one, before playing from dummy, you are starting to picture the full layout of the hand, and not just you and your partner's hand.

Interpret your opponent's lead

In the section on Defence, we'll be looking at lots of standard and not-so-standard (but correct) leads. Your job as declarer is to think about the lead your opponent has made and work out from what holding she has played. Still thinking, then place what you think is left in your other opponent's hand. From there, see how that might affect your plan.

Just using these two really basic thoughts, plan the play here:

Dealer South   ♠ Q53
Game All   ♥ A5
                                      ♦ 854
                                      ♣ KQJ93

```
      N
  W       E
      S
```

6♥ led

                                      ♠ AK2
                                      ♥ 9742
                                      ♦ AQ2
                                      ♣ 1074

N	E	S	W
–	–	1NT	NB
3NT			

You assume that West has five hearts, so East holds two. So, maybe you duck the first trick and win the continuation and then hope that East (who has no further hearts) holds A♣.

Unfortunately, that isn't good enough. You followed a rule (assume that the leader against NTs has a five-card suit) and then you switched off. Let's think more deeply.

You are missing K♥, Q♥, J♥ and 10♥. If West held any three out of these four cards, she should have led one. With any three honour cards at the head of your suit, you should lead one. Therefore, to have led fourth highest instead, you can conclude that West does not hold three honour cards, but only two. That leaves East with a doubleton heart – and both cards are honours.

Now, there is a far superior play available: you rise with A♥ at trick one. East will still be left with a heart honour and later either the suit will be blocked, or West will have to overtake/crash her partner's honour to keep on lead, allowing your 9♥ to become good. All of a sudden, the contract is 100 per cent safe. Here's the full deal.

Dealer South   ♠ Q53
Game All   ♥ A5
                   ♦ 854
                   ♣ KQJ93

	♠ 987		♠ J1064
	♥ KJ863	N	♥ Q10
	♦ 1063	W E	♦ KJ97
	♣ A8	S	♣ 652

                   ♠ AK2
                   ♥ 9742
                   ♦ AQ2
                   ♣ 1074

N	E	S	W
–	–	1NT	NB
3NT			

West leads 6♥, declarer hops up with A♥. Whichever card East plays, when West regains the lead with A♣, she faces an unpalatable choice. If she leads K♥ crashing East's Q♥ or 10♥, then dummy's 9♥ wins the fourth round; if West leads low to East, East wins, and has no heart left to lead.

Here's another situation where this simple thinking can help you enormously, again looking to thwart the defenders within their own long suit.

Dealer South
Love All

		♠ K73	
		♥ AQ63	
		♦ A952	
		♣ 84	

♠ 96			♠ QJ1054
♥ 1052	N		♥ 984
♦ Q76	W E		♦ J8
♣ A9752	S		♣ KJ10

		♠ A82	
		♥ KJ7	
		♦ K1043	
		♣ Q63	

N	E	S	W
–	–	1NT	NB
2C	NB	2D	NB
3NT			

West leads 5♣ to East's K♣; J♣ is returned. How does South know whether to rise with Q♣ or duck the trick?

Most good players do not lead a low card from a four- or five-card suit headed by the ten. From this holding, a top-of-rubbish lead is more normal. So, it seems likely that West holds A♣.

Since there is only one card lower than 5♣ unaccounted for, West cannot hold more than five clubs: East must hold at least three.

Using the old-fashioned Rule of 11, West's 5♣ lead suggests that there are six cards (11 – 5 = 6) higher than the 5♣ in the other three hands. You hold two, dummy one, and so East holds three cards higher than the five. Your only hope is to play for East to have started with ♣KJ10. On that basis, you should cover J♣ with Q♣. West wins, returns a club and East wins but, without any more clubs, East must relinquish control back to the declarer. In diamonds, declarer leads 3♦ from hand and, when West follows low, she puts in 9♦. East wins, but cannot put West back on lead again, and the contract is home.

Card placement at trick one

The bidding and opening lead often provide great insight into the shape of, and high-card positions within, your opponents' hands. Here's one of my all-time favourite examples:

```
Dealer West                    ♠ Q9843
N/S Game                       ♥ K7
                               ♦ Q65
                               ♣ 754

                                  ┌───────┐
                                  │   N   │
J♣ led                            │ W   E │
                                  │   S   │
                                  └───────┘

                               ♠ 6
                               ♥ AJ10962
                               ♦ 1042
                               ♣ AK3
```

N	E	S	W
–	–	–	1S
NB	1NT	2H	

All you have to do is to place each of the missing high cards in the correct hands. Right now; just from the bidding and the lead.

To help you: three key thoughts.

1) When you play a hand, always add up how many points you hold between you and dummy. If your opponents have bid, factor that into the likely placement of points.

2) When an opponent does not lead the suit she has called, it is often because, at the head of the suit, she holds the ace without the king, and does not wish to lead from it. An opponent might lead a singleton ahead of ace from ace-king, but usually you would cash one top trick before switching to your singleton.

3) When an opponent leads a low card in a suit, it means that she does not hold touching honour cards, such as: AK, KQJ, KQ10, QJ10, QJ9, etc., right down to 1098 or 1097. Instead, honour cards will be alone, or broken.

Back to the problem. Having placed the missing cards, what's your basic plan to bring home eight tricks?

Between your hand and dummy, you hold 19pts. West opened and East responded 1NT. For the moment, let's give East 7pts, and allocate West the remaining 14pts.

West led J♣, denying Q♣ (unless they are playing some arcane lead system). You can therefore place East with Q♣.

You are missing ♠AK. Since West did not lead a spade, you should assume that she does not hold both these cards. One of them is in the East hand. Let's assume, for the moment, it is K♠.

You are missing ♦AK. Since West did not lead a diamond, you should assume that one of them is in the East hand. As we've already placed East with Q♣ and K♠, it is less likely that East holds A♦, since that would give her 9pts and, in Acol, you are less likely to respond 1NT with 9pts unless you have a singleton or void in your partner's opened suit. Let's assume then East holds K♦.

Does West have a six-card spade suit? It's unlikely: she would probably have rebid 2S.

Who holds Q♥? This is the vital question on the hand.

West has ♠AJ, A♣ and J♦. Really, she needs to hold Q♥ to justify her opening bid.

Your plan should be to win trick one, and lead J♥. When West plays low, you run this card. As a result, you make six heart tricks and your ♣AK.

Here's the full deal:

```
Dealer West            ♠ Q9843
N/S Game               ♥ K7
                       ♦ Q65
                       ♣ 754
    ♠ AJ1072          ┌──────────┐         ♠ K5
    ♥ Q85             │    N     │         ♥ 43
    ♦ AJ              │  W   E   │         ♦ K9873
    ♣ J108            │    S     │         ♣ Q962
                      └──────────┘
                       ♠ 6
                       ♥ AJ10962
                       ♦ 1042
                       ♣ AK3
```

N	E	S	W
–	–	–	1S
NB	1NT	**2H**	

Notice that – by *thinking* – you discovered both the position of the high cards, and the basic shape of the hidden hands, a quarter of the way through trick one.

Remembering the key elements to think about, having seen dummy and your opponent's lead, have a go at planning this contract.

Dealer West   ♠ AK9
Love All   ♥ 7642
                              ♦ K108
                              ♣ 732

5♥ led

```
      N
  W       E
      S
```

East wins
with A♥

♠ J108742
♥ J
♦ Q76
♣ AKJ

N	E	S	W
–	–	–	1H
NB	2H	2S	NB
3S	NB	**4S**	

You and your partner hold 22pts between you, leaving E/W with 18pts. This looks like West has 12 or 13pts and East 5 or 6pts. E/W only have eight hearts between them, so it seems like a 5-3 fit.

West does not hold two touching heart honours since, with the suit having been agreed, she would have led one, even from ♥KQxxx. When East wins with A♥, you can place Q♥ in East's hand also. That would account for all her points, so West has both Q♠ and Q♣. On that basis, you should finesse West for Q♠ and play for the drop in clubs.

Does that work?

Dealer West   ♠ AK9
Love All   ♥ 7642
                  ♦ K108
                  ♣ 732

	♠ Q65		N		♠ 3

♠ Q65   ♠ 3
♥ K10853   W   E   ♥ AQ9
♦ AJ3   S   ♦ 9542
♣ Q8   ♣ 109654

                  ♠ J108742
                  ♥ J
                  ♦ Q76
                  ♣ AKJ

N	E	S	W
–	–	–	1H
NB	2H	2S	NB
3S	NB	**4S**	

Yes, it does – and your thin game contract is brought home successfully. It certainly looks more likely that West holds J♦ than East, so an overtrick is quite probable.

By the way, 1H is the best opening bid here, but even if West had opened 1NT, the lead is likely to have been the same, and all the conclusions would duly follow.

For more on this subject, I wholeheartedly recommend Mike Lawrence's brilliant book, *How To Read Your Opponents' Cards*, which first inspired me to pay much more attention to inferences from the opening lead, both positive and negative.

Compound NT Contracts

This is the term I give to hands which require two very distinctive actions in order to make sufficient tricks and in which you, as declarer, must decide in what order to undertake these plays. To illustrate the basic principle, let's take a look at an example.

Dealer North
Love All

♠ Q105
♥ 73
♦ A1054
♣ A976

Q♥ led

```
    N
 W     E
    S
```

♠ KJ4
♥ AK2
♦ QJ93
♣ K43

N	E	S	W
NB	NB	1D	1H
2C	NB	**3NT**	

To succeed, you will require spade tricks as well as diamond tricks. There are other matters of timing, but which of those two suits should you attack first?

If the diamond finesse is correct, it does not matter, but finesses should always be assumed to be wrong. Let's start to think about the hand.

We will assume that West began with a five-card heart suit, leaving East with three hearts. We are in danger of losing three heart tricks, A♠ and K♦, but the correct timing can avoid that. We should duck the first trick and win the continuation. That will leave East with just one heart. If we take the diamond finesse now and it loses, East will return that heart and clear the suit. Then, probably, West will hold A♠, win that, and cash her heart winners.

The crux here is that either player could hold and win with A♠, but only East can win K♦. For that reason, you want to take the diamond finesse at a point when East has no hearts left to lead. So, at trick three, declarer should play on spades first. West probably wins on the second round and clears the heart suit. Now, when you take the diamond finesse, when East wins, she has no hearts left to lead.

Here's the full deal:

Dealer North			♠ Q105
Love All			♥ 73
			♦ A1054
			♣ A976

	♠ A87				♠ 9632
	♥ QJ1094		N		♥ 865
	♦ 72	W		E	♦ K86
	♣ Q105		S		♣ J82

			♠ KJ4
			♥ AK2
			♦ QJ93
			♣ K43

N	E	S	W
NB	NB	1D	1H
2C	NB	**3NT**	

Play spades and diamonds the other way around, and declarer fails.

On this next deal, declarer's choice of action at trick one is entirely dependent on her plan for later.

Dealer South   ♠ 852
Love All   ♥ K5
         ♦ AQJ1076
         ♣ K7

```
              +-----------+
              |     N     |
7♠ led        |  W     E  |      East plays 10♠
              |     S     |
              +-----------+
```

         ♠ KQ3
         ♥ A632
         ♦ 532
         ♣ AJ2

N	E	S	W
–	–	1NT	NB
3NT			

Assuming that West started with five spades, East began with two and, since East can only contribute 10♠, West certainly holds A♠. The choice for declarer is to duck or win this trick. If declarer could ensure that only West will be on lead subsequently, then to win would be fine. However, here, declarer's plan is to finesse diamonds into the East hand. If East wins, it is essential that she cannot lead a spade through whatever South has left. For this reason, the clear-cut decision declarer should make is to duck this trick.

Dealer South   ♠ 852
Love All   ♥ K5
         ♦ AQJ1076
         ♣ K7

```
♠ AJ974       +-----------+       ♠ 106
♥ 74          |     N     |       ♥ QJ1098
♦ 98          |  W     E  |       ♦ K4
♣ Q543        |     S     |       ♣ 10986
              +-----------+
```

         ♠ KQ3
         ♥ A632
         ♦ 532
         ♣ AJ2

N	E	S	W
–	–	1NT	NB
3NT			

East returns 6♠ but, whether West wins or ducks this trick, when declarer finesses diamonds and East wins K♦, she has no spades left to return.

Creation of a new finesse

There are times when you know that taking a standard finesse will not work – and the missing honour will not drop – yet often I see players going ahead anyway. However, there are frequently opportunities to spurn the definitely losing finesse and instead create another finesse that might be successful.

Dealer West
Game All

```
                      ♠ AQ2
                      ♥ 1074
                      ♦ K62
                      ♣ KQ64
  ♠ 764                              ♠ 10985
  ♥ AQ983          N                 ♥ J
  ♦ Q73         W     E              ♦ 1085
  ♣ A2             S                 ♣ 109875
                      ♠ KJ3
                      ♥ K652
                      ♦ AJ94
                      ♣ J3
```

N	E	S	W
–	–	–	1H
NB	NB	1NT	NB
3NT			

West leads 8♥ to East's J♥ and declarer, counting out the heart suit based on West holding five, believes J♥ to be a singleton, so she ducks. East switches to 10♠. South counts three spade tricks, two clubs and no guaranteed heart trick, so she requires four diamond tricks if possible. N/S hold 27pts, East has shown up with 1pt, so West – who opened the bidding – is likely to have all the remaining 12pts. So there is no point taking the usual diamond finesse. While East cannot hold Q♦, she could easily hold 10♦, and this new finesse should be the one

South engineers. She leads J♦ from hand and, if West ducks, she runs it. If West covers, she wins with K♦ in dummy and now leads 2♦. When East plays low, South puts in 9♦ and this wins.

Obviously the club suit must be breached and, having done so, there may be value in eliminating clubs and spades from the West hand in case she holds 10♦ also, but the principle, I hope, is clear.

Morton's Fork Coup

Named after the tax-collecting John Morton, this coup offers a defender a choice to which neither answer is correct.

```
Dealer South              ♠ K7542
Love All                  ♥ Q
                          ♦ 98642
                          ♣ K5
       ♠ AJ 6                                    ♠ 1093
       ♥ 109862          ┌──────────┐            ♥ K7543
       ♦ K               │    N     │            ♦ QJ
       ♣ J1042           │  W   E   │            ♣ Q97
                         │    S     │
                         └──────────┘
                          ♠ Q8
                          ♥ AJ
                          ♦ A10753
                          ♣ A863
```

N	E	S	W
–	–	1D	NB
1S	NB	2C	NB
3D	NB	**3NT**	

West leads 10♥ and South realises that, having pushed out her diamond loser, she will still hold only eight tricks. When she does lose the diamond trick, E/W will continue hearts, leaving her with no stopper, and therefore no time to establish a spade trick.

Declarer has two extra chances. If she leads a spade and her opponents duck it, she will have sneaked through a spade trick and can then return to diamonds. Secondly, if the outstanding spades are 3-3 and East or West grab their A♠ without taking a spade honour, declarer will then have four spade tricks to go with her two heart tricks, two clubs and A♦.

So, giving herself the best chance of this, at trick two, declarer should lead 8♠ from hand and, sure enough, West is caught on Morton's Fork. If she rises with A♠, the contract makes, thanks to four spade tricks; if she ducks, the contract makes because declarer has made a spade trick and can now dislodge her diamond loser in comfort.

Creating entries

Vital in both NT and suit contracts, entries will often define your ability to establish your long suit. This first example occurs, in various forms, frequently in NT contracts.

Dealer North
Love All

	♠ AK52	
	♥ A32	
	♦ AQ10	
	♣ Q94	

♠ Q76		♠ J1093
♥ K10985	N	♥ 76
♦ J74	W E	♦ K985
♣ 87	S	♣ A53

	♠ 84	
	♥ QJ4	
	♦ 632	
	♣ KJ1062	

N	E	S	W
1S	NB	1NT	NB
3NT			

I often set this type of problem to my students, as I see players going wrong so frequently.

West leads 10♥ and declarer thoughtlessly tries to make a cheap trick by running it to her J♥ in hand. This works and South is very happy. She plays clubs, but East holds up until the final round. Now, when East returns a heart, whichever card South plays West beats it, and South can never get back into her hand to make her last two club tricks.

First of all, look at the heart suit: you will only make two tricks in hearts whatever you do. Secondly, your play to trick one is dependent on your plan for the hand. That should be to establish the club suit in your own hand and retain a certain entry to your hand in order to be able to enjoy the club winners. Hence, at trick one, you rise with A♥ in dummy, push out A♣ and, still holding ♥QJ, one of those cards will definitely provide you with access back to your hand. Simple.

This next hand reveals a 'secret' entry.

Dealer South
Love All

		♠ A543	
		♥ 1032	
		♦ 652	
		♣ 1043	

♠ J76			♠ 98
♥ 84	N		♥ K9765
♦ KQ109	W E		♦ A83
♣ QJ92	S		♣ 765

		♠ KQ102	
		♥ AQJ	
		♦ J74	
		♣ AK8	

N	E	S	W
–	–	2NT	NB
3NT			

Seduced by her two tens, North raises to 3NT (and also correctly rejects using Stayman with such a weak and balanced hand).

West leads K♦, East overtakes with A♦ and returns 8♦, and South is very relieved when West shows up with only four diamonds. At trick five, West leads Q♣ and now declarer realises that not only must the heart finesse be correct, but she must reach dummy twice to repeat the finesse.

Four-four fits often offer the chance to create an entry (or two, or three) and this one is no exception. South cashes ♠KQ, noting that the suit is dividing. She carefully leads 10♠ and overtakes with A♠, then takes the winning heart finesse. Due to her care, she can now play her 2♠ to dummy's 5♠ to repeat the finesse and bring home her contract.

The next hand was played by a friend of mine many years ago and demonstrates his Polish ambition in the auction and cool pragmatism in the play:

```
Dealer South            ♠ 853
Love All                ♥ 75432
                        ♦ 652
                        ♣ AJ

    ♠ 10642                             ♠ K97
    ♥ A986          N                   ♥ J10
    ♦ 103        W     E                ♦ 74
    ♣ Q104          S                   ♣ 986532

                        ♠ AQJ
                        ♥ KQ
                        ♦ AKQJ98
                        ♣ K7
```

N	E	S	W
–	–	2C	NB
2D	NB	4D	NB
5C*	NB	**6NT**	

After South's trump-setting jump to 4D, North's 5C is a cue-bid. South's decision to bid 6NT rather than 6D was simple: he didn't want me to play the hand.

West led A♥ and another, and declarer realised that only two entries to dummy for two spade finesses was likely to be enough. Unhesitatingly, he led 7♣ from hand and finessed with dummy's J♣. He took the winning spade finesse and then led K♣ to A♣ and took the spade finesse again.

The crux was that West holding Q♣ was a much better chance than East holding precisely a singleton or doubleton K♣. That was the correct play to develop an extra entry, and so, frightening as it may seem, that was what was done.

Yes, I know that if West rises with Q♣ on the first club trick, this defeats the contract. You would really have to be in the zone to find this defence.

Retaining entries

Entries are valuable things and, in a weak hand, they must be cherished. With a few satisfactory cards, some simple thought will often prove sufficient.

Dealer South

```
                        ♠ A108
                        ♥ Q762
                        ♦ K54
                        ♣ J93
  ♠ 65432                             ♠ 97
  ♥ A105          N                   ♥ K83
  ♦ QJ102     W       E               ♦ A87
  ♣ 2             S                   ♣ K8764
                        ♠ KQJ
                        ♥ J94
                        ♦ 963
                        ♣ AQ105
```

N	E	S	W
–	–	1NT	

West leads Q♦ and declarer considers the position. She has three spades, possibly a heart eventually, possibly a diamond, and three or four clubs. Deciding that West is less likely to hold A♦ than East, she ducks the lead, ducks also when West continues with J♦, and East wins the third round with A♦. East now switches to 9♠.

This is revealing. Attacking dummy's weakest suit – clubs – seems the more obvious switch. This suggests that East holds K♣ and does not want to lead from it when entries to dummy are short and J♣ sits to her right. It also suggests that she may well hold A♦ as well, since, without A♦, a diamond switch would seem reasonable too. How should you develop the club suit?

Winning in dummy with A♠, declarer can lead J♣ from the table and, when East plays low, South plays low from her hand also. But, crucially, South must not play 5♣. Instead, she should throw 10♣. Now, she can lead 9♣ and when East again plays low, declarer can drop 5♣. (You can play those two tricks the other way around too, of course.) As a result of this little bit of care, declarer is still in dummy to lead a club for the third time, finesse East's K♣ and make three spades and four clubs for her contract.

Detective work

I have written about counting and detective work many times, but so many students and players opt to guess that I had to try one more time. And, to finish this little section, a truly beautiful piece of detective work I read about just recently.

Somebody famous in the bridge world once announced: 'Two-way finesses are never guesses.' Clearly, that orator had never played bridge in the kitchens of some of my students.

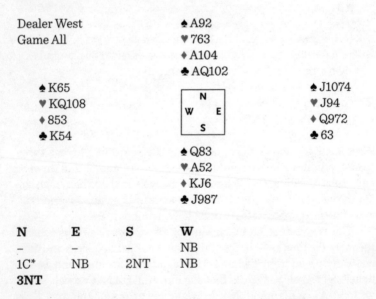

Dealer West
Game All

♠ A92
♥ 763
♦ A104
♣ AQ102

♠ K65
♥ KQ108
♦ 853
♣ K54

♠ J1074
♥ J94
♦ Q972
♣ 63

♠ Q83
♥ A52
♦ KJ6
♣ J987

N	E	S	W
–	–	–	NB
1C*	NB	2NT	NB
3NT			

North is too strong to open with a 12–14pt 1NT. With two tens, her hand is worth 15pts in no-trumps.

West led K♥. Hopefully, declarer has four club tricks, two diamonds, a heart and a spade. It looks like she will have to find who holds Q♦ and finesse them for it.

On trick one, East jettisons J♥ and declarer ducks this trick and the next, wins with A♥ and is pleased to find that East follows to the third round also.

At this point, *don't* take the diamond finesse.

Take the club finesse and, finding it correct, repeat. If West is lazy, on the fourth round, she may well throw away a diamond. East will probably cling to diamonds. Even this information may guide you to guess who holds Q♦.

At this point, *don't* take the diamond finesse.

As West only had four hearts, you can try to make a ninth trick an alternative way. Having finished in dummy with A♣, now lead 2♠ towards your Q♠ in hand. If East holds K♠, you'll make your ninth trick there. In fact, West wins, cashes her final heart, and gets off lead with another spade. If West is lazy, she may lead a diamond.

At this point, *don't* take the diamond finesse.

West seems to be producing a lot of high cards. What were they? Oh yes: K♠, ♥KQ, K♣ – that is 11pts. She passed originally, but if she also held Q♦, she would have had 13pts and would have opened the bidding. So, now you know that East holds Q♦.

Play 6♦ to A♦ and hook East's queen on the way back.

No guessing; just *thinking*.

This next hand is a delight.

Dealer South
E/W Game

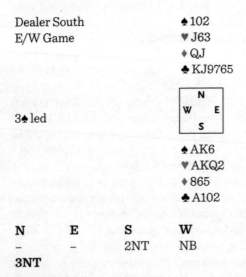

♠ 102
♥ J63
♦ QJ
♣ KJ9765

3♠ led

♠ AK6
♥ AKQ2
♦ 865
♣ A102

N	E	S	W
–	–	2NT	NB
3NT			

Clearly, all will depend on the club suit. Lose a trick there and the opponents will surely switch to diamonds and take four or five tricks quickly.

Let's think this through before making any quick decisions. Declarer should win the lead to avoid an immediate diamond switch, and then cash four rounds of hearts. On the third and fourth rounds, West discards low diamonds. This alone suggests that she is protecting her club suit, but there is a more compelling deduction: West's 3♠ lead marks her with a four-card suit (the only possible fifth-highest spade, 2♠, was in dummy) and she held only two hearts. This leaves her seven cards in clubs and diamonds. These must be dividing 4-3 since, if West held a five-card suit, surely she would have led that rather than a pretty poor four-card spade suit. Knowing that West holds at least three clubs allows declarer to lay down A♣ (East might hold the singleton Q♣) and then lead 10♣. If West does not cover, she runs it, knowing that it will win.

Here's the deal:

```
Dealer South          ♠ 102
E/W Game              ♥ J63
                      ♦ QJ
                      ♣ KJ9765

  ♠ Q973          ┌──────────┐      ♠ J854
  ♥ 104           │    N     │      ♥ 9875
  ♦ 10432         │ W     E  │      ♦ AK97
  ♣ Q84           │    S     │      ♣ 3
                  └──────────┘
                      ♠ AK6
                      ♥ AKQ2
                      ♦ 865
                      ♣ A102
```

N	E	S	W
–	–	2NT	NB
3NT			

By the way, if you're reading this, you're far too good to be bothering with old wives' tales, and one of the oldest – and most destructive – is this:

> With nine cards between the two hands, missing the queen, play for the drop.
> With eight cards between the two hands, missing the queen, finesse the queen.

If you have absolutely no other information, I suppose so. But, I mean *zero* information. Even the tiniest inference should guide you towards a play with better odds than those.

It's all about *thinking* and not about remembering rules.

Dummy Reversals

You make ruffs in the hand that is short in trumps, and preserve the trump length in the hand that is long in trumps, in order to be able to draw your opponents' trumps and keep control of the hand.

This is the case with the vast majority of bridge hands, and it is guidance broken at your peril. However, on some occasions, you will need to reverse which hand ends up with the longer trumps by the time it comes to draw them. This technique is known as a 'Dummy Reversal'.

Let's see it in action:

Dealer South
N/S Game

```
                         ♠ 10732
                         ♥ QJ7
                         ♦ KQ4
                         ♣ 1075
  ♠ AKJ96                              ♠ Q85
  ♥ 842            ┌─────────┐         ♥ 93
  ♦ 63          W │    N    │ E       ♦ 9752
  ♣ AQ8            │    S    │         ♣ J643
                   └─────────┘
                         ♠ 4
                         ♥ AK1065
                         ♦ AJ108
                         ♣ K92
```

N	E	S	W
–	–	1H	1S
2H	2S	3D*	NB
4H			

South's 3D is a frisky game-try, not promising four diamonds. Even so, North holds great cards in both partner's suits, and so accepts the invitation to game.

West leads ♠AK. Declarer has a spade and three clubs to lose. She could discard a club from dummy, but she will not have time to ruff the third club from hand there. Instead, declarer must seek to reverse the dummy, making North the master hand, and leaving it with the trump length.

South ruffs West's second spade, plays a heart to dummy's J♥ and ruffs a second spade in hand. She crosses to dummy's K♦ and ruffs dummy's final spade with a high trump. Declarer now has one trump in hand and two in dummy. She cashes her last top trump in hand, crosses to dummy with Q♦ and draws West's final trump with dummy's Q♥. Now, 4♦ is played to J♦ in hand and on A♦ declarer throws 5♣ from dummy.

Declarer has lost only one trick to date, and now she will lose only the two clubs remaining in dummy. Ten tricks made.

Here, declarer reduced her five trumps to only two (by ruffing spades three times), keeping three trumps in dummy for drawing trumps. This raises a key requirement for a dummy reversal: the trumps in the originally shorter holding must be sufficiently high to be able to control the trump suit and draw out opponents' trumps. If they are not high enough, a dummy reversal will probably not succeed.

It continues to amaze me how, on first glance, a contract which appears to be short of a trick suddenly becomes viable once you have looked at it the other way around.

Dealer North
N/S Game

	♠ A763	
	♥ KJ9	
	♦ A53	
	♣ K76	

♠ QJ9	N	♠ K10854
♥ 73	W E	♥ 842
♦ J974	S	♦ 82
♣ 10842		♣ J95

	♠ 2	
	♥ AQ1065	
	♦ KQ106	
	♣ AQ3	

N	E	S	W
1S	NB	2H	NB
2NT	NB	3D	NB
4H	NB	4NT	NB
5C	NB	5NT	NB
6C	NB	**7H**	

When North, by jumping to 4H, showed good cards in both hearts and diamonds, South launched into RKCB, and followed it with the king-asking 5NT. When North indicated K♣, South decided to risk 7H.

If declarer merely draws trumps and plays off her winners, the 4-2 diamond break will result in defeat. Is there a better line of play?

Because dummy contains three top trumps, providing hearts break 3-2 (roughly two-thirds of the time) the contract is completely safe.

West leads a trump – often the best option against a grand slam – and declarer prepares to reverse the dummy. She wins in dummy, cashes A♠ and ruffs 3♠ with a high trump in hand. She plays a diamond to A♦, and ruffs a second spade with high trump in hand. She plays a club to K♣ and ruffs dummy's final spade in hand, again with a high trump. Now, she plays 5♥ to dummy and draws the remaining trumps.

With dummy now the master hand, it contains only two diamonds and two clubs, both of which are covered by the high-card winners in the declarer's hand.

Again, declarer started with five trumps, but was reduced to two, making North the master hand – the advantage being that North did not have a fourth diamond to worry about losing.

The same thinking can be applied to hands where both the declarer and the dummy hold the same number of trumps but, played the traditional way, there seems to be a loser (or more) too many. Some players will find this technique easy, and see it immediately, while others struggle to envisage the hand played the wrong way around. The key, as ever, is to get into good habits and try to examine a hand from both angles (both the declarer playing the hand, and dummy playing the hand).

Dealer South
N/S Game

```
                    ♠ 732
                    ♥ AJ4
                    ♦ KJ10
                    ♣ QJ86

    ♠ K10                               ♠ Q986
    ♥ 109872          N                 ♥ K653
    ♦ 8752         W     E              ♦ 63
    ♣ 32              S                 ♣ 754

                    ♠ AJ54
                    ♥ Q
                    ♦ AQ94
                    ♣ AK109
```

N	E	S	W
–	–	1C	NB
3C	NB	**6C**	

South could not think of a good way of approaching the slam, so opted for a punt instead. West leads 10♥. From the declarer's perspective, she has three spade losers (or a heart and a spade). Looked at from the dummy's perspective, dummy has two spade losers, one of which could be pitched on declarer's fourth diamond. It is from that angle that the correct plan can be formed: to ruff two hearts in the South hand before drawing trumps.

Declarer wins the lead with A♥, ruffs a heart in hand. She crosses to K♦ and ruffs the last heart in hand. Now, she can draw all the trumps, followed by all the diamonds, discarding a spade from hand. She has lost no tricks, and only one losing spade remains in the new master hand – dummy.

Upside-down hands

If you play Transfers, or a conventional defence to 1NT, you should already know exactly what I mean by an upside-down hand. Yet I encounter players using Transfers who, when they come to play the hand, seem blind to the fact that a completely different approach is required. And, by the way, there are many defenders who misunderstand the situation also . . .

Dealer South
E/W Game

```
                          ♠ A9642
                          ♥ 83
                          ♦ K542
                          ♣ 73
   ♠ 7                    ┌─────────┐        ♠ QJ103
   ♥ KQJ10                │    N    │        ♥ 976
   ♦ J986                 │ W     E │        ♦ Q103
   ♣ K964                 │    S    │        ♣ AQ5
                          └─────────┘
                          ♠ K85
                          ♥ A542
                          ♦ A7
                          ♣ J1082
```

N	E	S	W
–	–	1NT	NB
2H*	NB	**2S**	

North's 2H was a standard red-suit Transfer, indicating a five-card spade suit with any number of points. West led K♥. Because dummy contains more trumps than declarer's hand, this must be played upside-down: despite the poor trump break, declarer can still prevail if she seeks to ruff diamonds in her own hand (the shorter trump holding) before drawing any trumps.

Notice that this is not a dummy reversal as declarer is using her trumps in the traditional way: long trump holding for drawing trumps, short trump holding for ruffing. It is merely using that technique upside-down.

South ducks the opening lead. West might continue hearts, trying to force the long trump holding in dummy to ruff – which would be good defence – or, if she suspected that declarer might want to ruff diamonds in her own hand, she might switch to a trump. Whatever West does, declarer can win, cash A♦ and K♦ and ruff a diamond in hand. Next she can ruff a heart in dummy (which gains her nothing – it is merely an entry) and seek to ruff her last diamond in hand. If East trumps in, it is with a natural trump trick anyway; if East ruffs low or not all, South can ruff. As a result, she makes three natural trump tricks, A♥, ♦AK and two diamond ruffs (or one ruff and an extra trump trick). Eight tricks, just made.

Dealer South　　　　　　♠ A2
E/W Game　　　　　　　♥ AQ102
　　　　　　　　　　　　♦ 42
　　　　　　　　　　　　♣ AJ983

```
♠ KQ7                                    ♠ J1096
♥ 985              N                     ♥ K76
♦ KQ86          W     E                  ♦ J10
♣ K64              S                     ♣ Q1075
```

　　　　　　　　　　　　♠ 8543
　　　　　　　　　　　　♥ J43
　　　　　　　　　　　　♦ A9753
　　　　　　　　　　　　♣ 2

N	E	S	W
–	–	–	1NT
2C*	NB	**2H**	

North's 2C overcall is Asptro, showing hearts and another suit, at least 5-4 distribution. South, with a weak hand and three-card support for partner's major and a singleton outside, bids 2H immediately, and this is passed out.

West correctly leads a trump and declarer must resist the temptation to finesse, needing to preserve two trumps in her hand for ruffing. She rises with A♥, cashes A♣ and ruffs a club, gets to dummy with A♠ and ruffs another club. Those five tricks, plus A♦ and two natural trump tricks, give her eight tricks.

All focus had to be on utilising the shorter trump hand's holding – usually dummy but, here again, declarer's hand. Even ducking the first round of trumps would lead to defeat. East would win and continue with a second trump.

Dealer South
Game All

		♠ A10832	
		♥ J64	
		♦ K53	
		♣ KQ	

♠ 64			♠ QJ7
♥ K9752			♥ Q108
♦ J1098	W E		♦ 76
♣ 63	S		♣ AJ1092

		♠ K95	
		♥ A3	
		♦ AQ42	
		♣ 8754	

N	E	S	W
–	–	1NT	NB
2H*	NB	2S	NB
3NT	NB	**4S**	

North's 2H is a standard Transfer leading to the type of everyday contract which, if played by North, would be made by all but the least experienced declarer. Here, South must not be distracted by thinking about diamond breaks, or when to lose her trump trick. All that needs to be done is for declarer to trump a heart in hand before the trumps are drawn. If West leads J♦, declarer should win in hand, and play A♥, followed by her 3♥. Whatever E/W do now, nothing can stop declarer from ruffing J♥ in hand, drawing two rounds of trumps, and bringing home her game.

Discarding losers from dummy

The vast majority of the time, your plan is to set up a long suit in dummy, planning to discard losers from your own hand. However, there are times when dummy contains no long suit but, with sufficient trumps in both hands, a loser can be discarded from dummy and then the low card in hand trumped in dummy. The key to these hands is often spotting the long suit in the first place!

Dealer East
N/S Game

```
                    ♠ K63
                    ♥ A865
                    ♦ Q4
                    ♣ Q753
  ♠ QJ104                          ♠ 987
  ♥ 73           N                 ♥ K2
  ♦ A1082     W     E              ♦ 9765
  ♣ J96          S                 ♣ A1082
                    ♠ A52
                    ♥ QJ1094
                    ♦ KJ3
                    ♣ K4
```

N	E	S	W
–	NB	1H	NB
3H	NB	**4H**	

West leads Q♠ against your 4H contract. Plan the play.

You have one loser in each suit and no long suit in dummy to establish, nor a shortage which can be utilised for ruffing. With the heart finesse wrong, the only avoidable loser seems to be the third round of spades.

Finding your long suit may be the problem here but, with two diamonds in dummy and three in hand, this extra diamond can be used to discard a spade from the table. You will need to retain an entry into the hand which contains the long suit – your hand. Win trick one with K♠, play ♦Q4 and, when West wins – probably on the second round – you can use A♠ to return to hand later and discard a low spade from dummy on K♦. Later, when it is safe, you can ruff the last spade from your hand in dummy.

Dealer North
Game All

                    ♠ KJ42
                    ♥ 7543
                    ♦ K52
                    ♣ J4

    ♠ A3   ♠ 76
    ♥ QJ10   N   ♥ 9862
    ♦ Q106   W   E   ♦ J987
    ♣ AQ1082   S   ♣ 975

                    ♠ Q10985
                    ♥ AK
                    ♦ A43
                    ♣ K63

N	E	S	W
NB	NB	1S	2C
2S	NB	**4S**	

West leads Q♥. From the auction, declarer can place most missing high cards in West's hand. Declarer sees that with a spade, diamond and two clubs to lose, she must create an extra trick for a quick discard, and this can be achieved in clubs, allowing her to pitch a diamond loser from dummy which, later, will allow her to ruff her third round of diamonds on the table. But, how should declarer play the club suit?

Since West is very likely to hold A♣, the best chance is to win the lead, and lead a low club. You cannot afford to cross to dummy with K♦ since this would open up the suit to a successful attack from West when she wins her first and second club tricks. If West holds A♣ and East Q♣, you are doomed, but the bidding suggests this isn't likely. West must rise with Q♣ to prevent J♣ winning and now, even if she switches to a diamond, declarer can win and lead a club to J♣, pushing out A♣. K♣ in hand is now established on which to throw a low diamond from dummy. Trumps can be drawn and the diamond ruff made later.

Endplays

As the name suggests, these are plays that often occur towards the end of the hand, where through design or good fortune a defender is left with a decision to which all answers give the declarer an extra trick or tricks.

In theory, an opponent can be endplayed from the opening lead, but this section is about creating the correct conditions to attempt to endplay an opponent.

The most common type of endplay involves the declarer eliminating the possibility of the opponent getting off lead safely, hence the name: elimination endplay.

Elimination endplays in suit contracts

In suit contracts, you have the advantage of trumps. The most powerful endplay element is that if an opponent leads a suit in which you hold no cards in either your hand or dummy, you are then able to make a 'ruff and discard' – allowing you to trump in one hand and throw away a loser in the other. Defenders don't want to do this, of course, so you must force them to lead the suit you want them to play or concede a dreaded ruff and discard.

In order for an endplay to work, you need to ensure that your opponent(s) is thrown on lead at just the right moment:

- when all trumps have been drawn from opponents' hands (or, occasionally, when just the opponent you plan to be endplayed has no trumps remaining);
- when you have eliminated, or stripped, any other suit(s) in which your opponent may be able to get off lead safely.

Also, that you identify and time the use of an 'exit card' – a card with which you can force your opponent to win the trick, leaving her unable to get off lead safely.

```
Dealer South          ♠ J32
Game All              ♥ AQ963
                      ♦ 85
                      ♣ AK3
    ♠ 9875                            ♠ 1064
    ♥ 2            ┌─────────┐        ♥ 105
    ♦ KJ43         │   N     │        ♦ 109762
    ♣ QJ98         │ W   E   │        ♣ 652
                   │   S     │
                   └─────────┘
                      ♠ AKQ
                      ♥ KJ874
                      ♦ AQ
                      ♣ 1074
```

South ends in 6H on Q♣ lead from West. Declarer sees that she has a certain club loser and a diamond finesse. Rather than taking the finesse (which, here, loses), she plans an endplay.

Many readers will spot what to do immediately, but let's take it slowly.

Declarer notes that West's Q♣ lead almost certainly promises J♣ (it could, possibly, be a singleton). Since declarer holds 10♣, this can be her exit card to throw West on lead later. First, she must set up the position, so that West is forced to lead a diamond. To do this, any safe means of getting off lead must be eliminated.

Declarer wins the lead, and draws two rounds of trumps, which removes trumps from the opponents' hands. Next, she cashes ♠AKQ. This removes the spades from both her hand and dummy. At this point, she cashes her remaining top club and plays 10♣. West is forced to win with J♣ and now faces an unpalatable choice. If West plays a club or a spade, declarer can ruff in dummy and discard Q♦ from her hand. So, West must lead a diamond, hoping that her partner holds Q♦. As a result, South makes both diamond tricks and her contract.

Notice that having trumps left in both dummy and her hand meant that an opponent leading a suit in which declarer was void in both hands permitted a ruff and discard.

That was a very simple example. Let's illustrate how declarer may have to work harder to create a similar position.

Dealer South   ♠ AJ64
Game All   ♥ KQ7
                   ♦ A85
                   ♣ 832

   ♠ KQ109   ♠ 8732
   ♥ 32   **N**   ♥ 65
   ♦ 32   **W**   **E**   ♦ J10976
   ♣ KJ765   **S**   ♣ 109

                  ♠ 5
                  ♥ AJ10984
                  ♦ KQ4
                  ♣ AQ4

N	E	S	W
–	–	1H	NB
1S	NB	3H	NB
4D*	NB	4NT	NB
5C	NB	5D*	NB
6H			

North's 4D was an Advance Cue-Bid (see page 121), and South's 5D after North's RKCB response asked for the trump queen. The response of 6H showed the trump queen but denied any other king.

    West leads K♠. South has one certain club loser (the third round) and a club finesse to take. To avoid this, South must plan to force West to lead a club to her. The K♠ lead promises Q♠, so dummy's J♠ should be the exit card. South wins A♠ and ruffs a low spade in hand immediately. She should draw a round of trumps to dummy's K♥ and ruff a second low spade in hand. This leaves only J♠ remaining in dummy. Declarer must draw the last trumps before playing out three rounds of diamonds finishing in dummy. This eliminates the diamond suit from both her own hand and dummy. Now, she plays J♠ and, instead of trumping it, discards her 4♣ from hand. This loser-on-loser play ensures that West must win. If West could play a diamond or if she leads a spade, declarer can trump with dummy's final trump and discard Q♣ from hand; if she leads a club, the finesse is taken for declarer, and her slam is made.

    Notice that, if South had not ruffed the two low spades in dummy but left them there, when West won her Q♠ she could have got off lead safely with another spade and declarer would have had to rely on the losing club finesse. The ruffing of the low spades in hand ensured that the outside suits were correctly eliminated, and guaranteed that West had no safe way of getting off lead.

Partial elimination

In the example above, the trump suit broke 2-2, but what, you may ask, if the trumps had broken badly? If West had held length in trumps, it would have been unlikely (but not impossible) that you could endplay her, but if East had held the length, you would have had to attempt a 'Partial Elimination' in order to succeed.

Here is a similar example but, this time, the trumps break poorly.

Dealer South
Game All

	♠ AJ64	
	♥ KQ7	
	♦ A85	
	♣ 832	

♠ KQ109		♠ 8732
♥ 3	N	♥ 652
♦ 9632	W E	♦ J107
♣ KJ76	S	♣ 1095

	♠ 5	
	♥ AJ10984	
	♦ KQ4	
	♣ AQ4	

N	E	S	W
–	–	1H	NB
1S	NB	3H	NB
4D	NB	4NT	NB
5C	NB	5D	NB
6H			

Declarer makes the same plan as before but, this time, when the trumps do not break, she must change her plan somewhat. The key is that, often, if the hand you plan to endplay is the one without any further trumps, you can still succeed.

South wins the K♠ lead with A♠ and ruffs a low spade in hand, using 8♥. She draws a round of trumps by playing 4♥ to 7♥ and ruffs a second low spade in hand. She cashes a top trump and sees the bad break, but it is West who has no further trumps. Crucially, she now leaves the last trump outstanding in the East hand. This is because she must leave a trump in dummy to ensure that a ruff and discard ensues if West tries to get off lead with a suit in which declarer holds no cards in either her hand or dummy.

Declarer now cashes three diamonds. If East can ruff one of these, declarer will be defeated, but the odds are in declarer's favour since, crucially, West did not overcall 1S, so it seems that the spades are 4-4. Having played all the diamonds, again finishing in dummy, declarer leads J♠ and discards 4♣ from hand. West is similarly endplayed because if she gives a ruff and discard, dummy's trump is higher than East's and so the discard can be achieved in the South hand. Declarer then draws East's final trump.

Another definition of a partial elimination endplay is when the stripping of the side suits is incomplete, but sufficient to endplay the opponent into whose hand you will exit.

```
Dealer South              ♠ J8752
Game All                  ♥ A2
                          ♦ A732
                          ♣ 42

        ♠ Q6              N           ♠ K
        ♥ QJ1097      W       E       ♥ 8543
        ♦ J6              S           ♦ Q1095
        ♣ Q1075                       ♣ J983

                          ♠ A10943
                          ♥ K6
                          ♦ K84
                          ♣ AK6
```

N	E	S	W
–	–	1S	NB
3S	NB	4NT	NB
5H	NB	**6S**	

South has somewhat punted this slam and will need both skill and luck to succeed. Critically, there is really only one chance, and that must be taken. West leads Q♥ and declarer assesses that she has one trump loser (two if West holds all three) and a diamond loser. There appears to be no possible way to succeed, but a partial elimination endplay will lead to success.

Declarer wins trick one, cashes A♠ – relieved that both opponents do follow – and then sets about eliminating the side suits as far as possible. The other top heart is cashed, then ♣AK and 6♣ is ruffed in dummy and, finally, A♦ and K♦. This seems odd, but 8♦ or 7♦ were never going to create a trick. Declarer exits by playing a trump. West wins and the partial elimination proves sufficient because West has no more diamonds. When West leads a club or a heart, declarer ruffs in dummy and pitches her last diamond from hand.

If the diamonds are 3-3, or the hand with the winning heart still holds a diamond, declarer would fail, but there is no better chance available.

Elimination endplays in no-trump contracts

An endplay in no-trumps is similar to that in a suit contract but without the ability to form a ruff and discard situation. For this reason, your elimination (or stripping) of your opponents' side suits becomes even more vital, yet often only a partial elimination is possible . . .

Dealer West
Game All

```
              ♠ 875
              ♥ AK3
              ♦ 752
              ♣ Q1094
♠ KQJ104                      ♠ 96
♥ Q7          N               ♥ J10965
♦ KJ3       W   E             ♦ 10986
♣ 765         S               ♣ 82
              ♠ A32
              ♥ 842
              ♦ AQ4
              ♣ AKJ3
```

N	E	S	W
–	–	–	1S
NB	NB	2NT	NB
3NT			

South's 2NT overcall in the protective position shows 18–21pts; North raises to game. West leads K♠ and declarer counts her tricks: one spade; two hearts; one diamond and four clubs. There is only one card which might make a ninth trick and that is Q♦. However, North-South hold 27pts between them so, for East to hold K♦, West must have opened with only 10pts. This is possible, especially if West started with six spades but, at the moment, the count strongly suggests that West holds K♦.

In NT contracts, the most common suit to utilise for an exit card is the suit originally led by the opposition, and so it is here. South ducks the first lead, but wins West's Q♠ continuation. This is vital as declarer plans to use her final spade as an exit later. As East has followed to two rounds of spades, West is marked with no more than a five-card spade suit and now, almost certainly, K♦.

Declarer cashes four rounds of clubs, noting that West discards J♦ on the fourth round. She next cashes ♥AK, observing West drop Q♥. Declarer should now imagine West as holding three winning spades, plus ♦Kx. To succeed, South exits with her final spade. West takes her three tricks but must then lead from her ♦K3, ensuring South makes two diamond tricks and her contract.

Notice that the elimination of the heart suit was only partial, but it was sufficient.

An endplay is often required when there are no entries to dummy, as witnessed here.

Dealer East   ♠ Q1052
Game All   ♥ J2
               ♦ J943
               ♣ J95

♠ 8743		♠ K9
♥ 74	N	♥ KQ1098
♦ 8762	W E	♦ 105
♣ 764	S	♣ K1083

               ♠ AJ6
               ♥ A653
               ♦ AKQ
               ♣ AQ2

N	E	S	W
–	1H	Dbl	NB
1S	NB	2NT	NB
3NT			

West leads 7♥ and South, despite holding 24pts in her hand and 5pts in dummy, can count only six top tricks. If she concedes a trick to K♠ or K♣, East will win this and cash four heart tricks to defeat the contract. If only declarer could reach dummy to take the black suit finesses which, from the bidding, are marked as winning. Instead, however, declarer must set up a position to embarrass East.

South ducks the lead and K♥ continuation, winning the third round of hearts. West has followed to two rounds of hearts so East started with a five-card suit. South cashes ♦AKQ, and exits with her final heart. East wins this and takes her last heart trick on which, crucially, South should discard Q♣ to ensure that later, whichever suit East chooses to play, declarer can win in dummy. While there, South should cash J♦ and then lead 10♠ or Q♠ to take the spade finesse twice for two extra tricks.

Once again, the exit has been made in the suit that was originally led.

Endplays in no-trump contracts sometimes require courage to attempt the expert play rather than settle for the simple social bridge player option. Your chances will be boosted if you pay close attention to your opponents' actions, and try to interpret them with some card reading, or 'discard interpretation'.

Dealer South
Game All

		♠ K1063	
		♥ 1075	
		♦ AQ85	
		♣ 102	

♠ J2　　　　　　　　　　　　　　　　　　♠ Q9754
♥ QJ864　　　　　　　N　　　　　　　♥ K3
♦ 732　　　　　　W　　E　　　　　♦ 104
♣ K86　　　　　　　　S　　　　　　♣ J975

		♠ A8	
		♥ A92	
		♦ KJ96	
		♣ AQ43	

N	E	S	W
–	–	1D	NB
1S	NB	2NT	NB
3D*	NB	**3NT**	

North's 3D bid is forcing, indicating three- or four-card diamond support and a weakness in one or both of the unbid suits.

West leads 6♥. As discussed earlier, declarer should assume a five-card suit has been led but, when East wins with K♥ and returns 3♥ – her lowest – this confirms it. So, South must either finesse East for K♣ or form an endplay. There is no evidence from E/W's silence in the bidding who might hold K♣, so on what basis should South make a decision?

The first inference to be drawn is that with a queen-high heart suit, West is likely to have an outside entry or, being so weak, she might have opted to lead the other unbid suit, clubs.

Declarer should delay her decision a little longer. She wins the second round of hearts with A♥ and now plays off four rounds of diamonds. West probably discards 6♣ on the fourth round. East first discards a low spade. This discard is sometimes called the 'spare fifth' – a fifth card in a side-suit is usually easy to throw away. East may ponder a little longer over her second discard. She may well throw a second spade. This suggest two things:

She feels that by throwing a second spade, the declarer will not play her for Q♠; by refusing to throw a club, it suggests that she is protecting J♣, rather than K♣, since you only require one other card to protect a king, whereas to protect a jack, you need three other cards.

These are only *inferences* you can take from your opponents' actions, but they are surprisingly accurate.

Putting this information together: if East holds five spades, West only has two. West is protecting K♣; East J♣. This leaves West with ♥QJ8 and ♣Kx. On that basis, the endplay seems more likely to succeed than the finesse. Declarer should cash A♠ and K♠ and exit with dummy's last heart.

West duly takes her three hearts and must lead from ♣K8 to South's ♣AQ.

When you opt to try for an endplay and it doesn't work, you will sometimes look very silly, because perhaps a straightforward finesse would have done the job just fine. However, as you strive to play bridge well, occasional humiliation must be expected. I've had a lifetime of it.

Squeezes

There are many beautiful squeezes: double squeezes, compound squeezes, criss-cross squeezes, etc., which bring home seemingly absolutely impossible contracts but, frankly, these are – and should remain – the territory of international players with the ability to form an accurate idea of the distributions of all four hands and still have the brain capacity to plot and execute a coherent plan to create an extra trick from nowhere.

For club and social bridge players, there are squeezes which are within your grasp, and it is these which we will examine in this section.

Most squeezes require that, as declarer, you have lost all the tricks you can afford to lose before putting strain on the opposition. This is sometimes called 'rectifying the count', sometimes, 'loser reduction', but I prefer to think of it as taking the slack out of the end position. If the opponent – or, occasionally, opponents – only have valuable cards left, then whatever they throw is likely to be fatal to them. If you have two losers and can only afford one, make sure that you lose that one early on, to leave yourself with just the loser you cannot afford. Now, the squeeze will bite.

A genuine squeeze exists when an opponent (sometimes both) cannot stop either one threat – or 'menace' – or another from becoming a winner. Sometimes these menaces exist by right; other times, you must create them in order to form the squeeze. As is the case with establishing suits, careful control of entries must be exercised at all times to ensure that you can reach a card which has become established.

Let's look at a simple example to illustrate this:

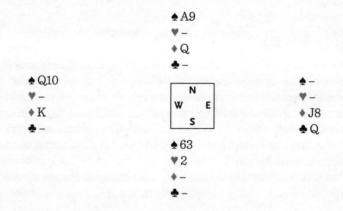

The first ten tricks of the hand have been played and we are in the three-card ending. South is playing with hearts as trumps and has lost all the tricks she can afford. She has 2♥ – the last trump – which is a trick, and dummy's A♠, but neither dummy's 9♠ or Q♦ are winners, since West has those two cards beaten. However, both these cards are menaces – they *could* become winners if the opponent protecting them releases that protection.

The good news is that South is on play and, when she leads her last trump, West must decide what to discard before declarer decides what she wants to throw away from the table. East is out of the hand by now, holding irrelevant cards.

When South leads her 2♥, West is genuinely squeezed.

If she throws her K♦, declarer pitches 9♠ from dummy, leaving A♠ and Q♦ as winners. If she throws 10♠, declarer pitches Q♦ from dummy, and now ♠A9 are both winners.

Notice that this deal illustrates a position where the declarer has:

- lost all the tricks she can afford;
- two cards which *could* become winners – these are the menaces;
- the entries to enjoy whichever card becomes a winner.

In the examples that follow, we will see both positions that pre-exist and that, with care, you can exploit, and positions that must be developed in order to create the conditions for the squeeze to bite – mainly, the creation of menaces, and the retention of entries with which to enjoy them.

I have often heard defenders claiming that they were squeezed, and sometimes declarers claiming that they have squeezed their opponents, but usually this was a more prosaic bridge play called *Throwing Away the Wrong Card*. The whole point of a squeeze – a real squeeze – is that whichever card your opponent throws will be the wrong card.

There is a real bridge term, a 'Pseudo Squeeze', which is when an opponent genuinely thinks they are squeezed but, unbeknownst to them, there is a safe card they could safely discard. The time when that occurs most frequently is when you have a long trump suit and, for want of any other idea, you play off all your trumps and hope that something good happens. Not only does this look extremely professional, but quite often something good really does happen!

Playing off your long trump suit

You may know that you have a completely unavoidable loser, but your opponents may not. Rather than conceding pusillanimously, play your trumps off and see what they discard. By the way, it will be your final trump – the one that hurts you to play – which will hurt your opponents.

Dealer West
Game All

♠ 932
♥ J85
♦ AK742
♣ 63

♠ 4
♥ AKQ1093
♦ QJ3
♣ 987

```
      N
  W       E
      S
```

♠ 76
♥ 742
♦ 109
♣ QJ10542

♠ AKQJ1085
♥ 6
♦ 865
♣ AK

N	E	S	W
–	–	–	1H
NB	NB	2S	3H
4D*	NB	**6S**	

South's jump-overcall in the protective position is strong (page 172), North's 4D bid is a Fit non-jump (page 156) and South's 6S bid is just a wild punt. However, when dummy hits the baize, declarer does have eleven tricks, but both a heart and a diamond loser seem inevitable.

West leads ♥AK and South trumps the second round. She draws two rounds of trumps and thinks about giving up. Instead, she cashes ♣AK and plays off her spades. West slowly comes under pressure. West must hold on to Q♥ to stop dummy's J♥ from becoming a winner. She must also preserve ◆QJ3 since, if she throws one of those, all dummy's diamonds become good.

This is a chance to emphasise a key term in squeeze play. Dummy's J♥ and her third diamond are 'menaces'. Neither is a trick yet but, if West throws away the card preventing them from becoming winners, then they are established. It is integral to a proper squeeze that there are two menaces, so one opponent (or sometimes both) becomes squeezed between protecting those two menaces from becoming tricks.

Here, as declarer plays off her trumps, West can safely throw away her last club and her ♥1093 but, when South leads her final trump, West is left with this:

West
♠ –
♥ Q
◆ QJ3
♣ –

What can she discard? If she throws Q♥, declarer discards 7◆ from dummy, and ◆AK and Q♥ are all winners. If West throws 3◆, declarer pitches J♥ from dummy and then scores her A◆, K◆ and 7◆.

Whatever West throws is wrong: she has been properly squeezed.

The beauty of this play is that you do not even need to know that you are doing it. It just happens.

Dealer West   ♠ AJ43
Game All   ♥ J2
                 ♦ J109
                 ♣ AK104

♠ 10		♠ 97
♥ AQ743	N	♥ 1096
♦ AK6	W E	♦ 8753
♣ QJ32	S	♣ 9765

                 ♠ KQ8652
                 ♥ K85
                 ♦ Q42
                 ♣ 8

N	E	S	W
–	–	–	1H
Dbl	NB	**4S**	

On this deal, if you manage a basic count of the key defender's hand, you can anticipate that you might get lucky.

West leads A♦, and declarer can see two diamond losers and, since the opening bid marks West with A♥, two heart losers also. If either hand holds ♣QJ doubleton or ♣QJx, an extra trick might be found in clubs.

West continues with K♦ and 6♦ and South wins the third round. She draws trumps, noticing that West started with a singleton. This suggests that West holds length in clubs also. If the club honours are divided, you cannot get home but, if West holds them both, a simple squeeze will bite. Play off a total of five rounds of trumps. West will discard three hearts and a low club. On the sixth and final trump, West is squeezed, holding:

West
♠ –
♥ AQ
♦ –
♣ QJ3

If she throws a club, all dummy's clubs are good; if she throws Q♥, you must now lead a club. If West plays low, you have to take the deep finesse with 10♣; if West splits her club honours, you win and exit with a heart. Now, West must lead from ♣Q3 and you take the finesse that way. Very difficult, I agree, but finding such plays is what distinguishes the top bridge players from the ordinary.

Isolating the menace

It is integral to a squeeze that you hold two menaces between which you place an opponent in a nasty – indeed, impossible – position. Sometimes, to achieve this, you will have to ensure that a menace cannot be guarded by both opponents. If it can, no one will be squeezed.

Dealer South
Love All

	♠ J854	
	♥ 1082	
	♦ A96	
	♣ AQ5	
♠ KQ1093		♠ A76
♥ 73	N	♥ 654
♦ 1082	W E	♦ 743
♣ K109	S	♣ 8762
	♠ 2	
	♥ AKQJ9	
	♦ KQJ5	
	♣ J43	

N	E	S	W
–	–	1H	1S
2S*	Dbl	3D	NB
4H	NB	4NT	NB
5H	NB	**6H**	

North's 2S bid over West's 1S overcall indicated an opening hand with three-card heart support – a slight overbid – and South then let rip and ended in a shaky small slam. West leads K♠ and then switches to a trump. Whether or not the club finesse is winning, unless West started with exactly ♣Kx, South still has a club loser to avoid. Clearly, J♣ in her own hand is a menace, but she needs another and dummy's

J♠ is it. However, from the bidding and the lead, it looks as if East holds A♠, so if South tries running the trumps, West will be able to discard her Q♠ safely. For the squeeze to bite, South must isolate the menace in West's hand. To do this, she must seek to ruff out East's A♠ – from the bidding, she knows that East started with no more than three spades – so that only West can stop dummy's J♠ from becoming a winner. Let's play the hand.

South wins West's trump switch in dummy with 10♥ and leads 5♠, ruffing in her hand. She draws two more rounds of trumps and plays 5♦ to A♦. Now, 8♠ is led, East's A♠ appears and declarer ruffs this with her last trump. This has removed East's ability to protect spades and all the pressure lies with West. Declarer takes the club finesse and Q♣ wins. She comes back to hand and plays off her diamonds. When South plays her final diamond, West is left with:

West

♠ Q

♥ –

♦ –

♣ K10

If West throws Q♠, dummy's J♠ becomes a winner. If West pitches 10♣, declarer throws J♠ from dummy and cashes A♣ felling West's K♣ and making J♣ her twelfth trick.

Notice that declarer kept A♣ in dummy until the end. There is no point having menaces if, when one becomes good, you don't have an entry to reach it!

Creating a menace

This is really just an extension of the play above but, here, there is no menace to begin with; you conjure one up. The good news is that this is not as tough as it sounds. Really, you are just trying to establish a long suit, but run out of entries.

Dealer South   ♠ J83
Game All   ♥ 104
                      ♦ AQ6
                      ♣ 97532

♠ AK52   ♠ Q1097
♥ 5   ┌─────────┐   ♥ 632
♦ K1084   │   N   │   ♦ 972
♣ J1084   │ W   E │   ♣ AKQ
                     │   S   │
                     └─────────┘
                      ♠ 64
                      ♥ AKQJ987
                      ♦ J53
                      ♣ 6

N	E	S	W
–	–	4H	

Not only has South's ambitious 4H opener resulted in a decent contract, but it has talked E/W out of bidding their making 4S contract. Clearly, South has seven hearts and two diamonds to win, but where on earth can she find two menaces with which to threaten an opponent? Her J♦ is one and, if constructed correctly, a club in dummy may be another. Let's observe the play.

West leads ♠AK and continues with 5♠ to East's Q♠. South ruffs. Immediately, she gives up a club. East wins and leads a trump. Declarer wins in dummy with 10♥ and ruffs a club in hand. She takes the diamond finesse which holds, and she ruffs another club, watching East play A♣. So, dummy's 9♣ has now become a menace. It looks like West holds both K♦ and J♣ so when South plays off all her trumps, West will be squeezed. Sure enough, on South's last trump, West holds:

West
♠ –
♥ –
♦ K10
♣ J

If she throws J♣, dummy's 9♣ is a winner; if she discards a diamond, both A♦ and J♦ are now winners. Slam made.

Notice that, if dummy had held one more entry than it did, declarer could have made the hand by losing a club and ruffing three clubs in hand so that dummy's fifth club was established. Declarer lacked the entries for that line, but had sufficient for a squeeze instead.

Squeezes in no-trump contracts

Finally, a quick look at squeezes in no-trump contracts. These can almost be distilled to the advice that, if you can't see enough tricks, try playing off your solid long suit before deciding what to do next. However, let's make it seem and sound a little more studied and professional than that.

Dealer West
N/S Game

```
                    ♠ AK62
                    ♥ 643
                    ♦ A87
                    ♣ J75

  ♠ J1085                           ♠ 93
  ♥ AKJ10          N                ♥ 9752
  ♦ 43          W     E             ♦ 9652
  ♣ K108           S                ♣ 964

                    ♠ Q74
                    ♥ Q8
                    ♦ KQJ10
                    ♣ AQ32
```

N	E	S	W
–	–	–	1C
NB	NB	Dbl	NB
2S	NB	2NT	NB
3NT			

Playing five-card majors, West opened a better minor 1C, and N/S soon reached 3NT. West led K♥ (see page 61) and East made a count signal with 9♥, suggesting that she held four cards in the heart suit. This allowed West to play three further heart winners. At trick five, West switched to J♠. Declarer has three spades, four diamonds and a club but, unless the spades split 3-3, seemingly no chance of a ninth trick as the bidding has clearly marked West with K♣.

However, if West holds both K♣ and length in spades, a squeeze will bite. All declarer needs to do now is to run off her solid diamond suit, and watch for West's discomfort. Having won the spade switch with Q♠ in hand, South can cash one top spade and then play four rounds of diamonds. On the final diamond, West is holding:

West
♠ 108
♥ –
♦ –
♣ K10

If she throws a spade, then both remaining spades in dummy will be good; if she ditches 10♣, K♣ is bared and declarer will score both A♣ and Q♣.

You can often tell when a squeeze is about to work: there is growing concern emanating from every pore of the defender about to be put under unbearable pressure and, sometimes, defenders pull faces, groan, moan or mutter. But a word of warning here: many bridge players find it very hard to foresee what will happen on the trick beyond the one they are playing, and also to remember which cards are winners, so do not be surprised if a defender blithely throws away a winning card, unaware that she is being squeezed, having completely lost track of the hand ...

Loser Exchanges

There are many situations in bridge where is it preferable to lose a trick to one opponent rather than another, to take a risk in one suit opposed to another, to sacrifice a trick in order to sever your opponents' communications, even simply to develop extra tricks or preserve your trump quality. Here are some of the key plays about which you should be aware.

Dealer South
E/W Game

♠ Q5
♥ 1065
♦ J74
♣ A7542

```
    N
W       E
    S
```

♠ 964
♥ AKQ74
♦ AK5
♣ K10

N	E	S	W
–	–	1H	1S
2H	NB	**4H**	

West leads ♠AK, East playing 3♠, then 8♠. West now leads J♠. What should South do?

It looks like West started with five spades and East with three but, when North ruffs with 10♥, East over-ruffs with J♥ and declarer goes on to lose a diamond trick.

Why did East signal like that? Perhaps E/W are playing Reverse signals, or East played the card nearest her thumb, or decided to get tricky. You can't rely on your opponents being honest with you. Instead, South should reason that West could have six spades and, therefore, to try to ruff the third round is a risk. Much less dangerous would be to ruff the third round of diamonds. To this end, declarer should not ruff the third spade, but instead discard 4♦ from dummy. Later, declarer can play A♦, K♦ and safely ruff 5♦ in dummy. Here's the full deal:

Dealer South
E/W Game

		♠ Q5	
		♥ 1065	
		♦ J74	
		♣ A7542	
♠ AKJ1062			♠ 83
♥ 92	N		♥ J83
♦ 983	W E		♦ Q1062
♣ J3	S		♣ Q986
		♠ 974	
		♥ AKQ74	
		♦ AK5	
		♣ K10	

N	E	S	W
NB	NB	1H	1S
2H	NB	**4H**	

Even if West leads a fourth spade, South can pitch a second diamond from dummy, and over-ruff East in hand. Now, declarer must play A♦, ruff 5♦ and draw the trumps, saving cashing K♦ until later. Again, she is home safely.

You may argue that West should have made a weak jump-overcall of 2S – and so she might – but opponents don't do what you might expect of them, and you still have to remain alert.

Loser-on-loser to protect trumps

This is a really easy hand which I often set to students – and find
that they go down...

Dealer East

N/S Game

			♠ 62
			♥ J542
			♦ AKQ
			♣ 9863

♠ J74
♥ K93
♦ 64
♣ AKJ105

```
    N
 W     E
    S
```

♠ 105
♥ 10876
♦ J10983
♣ 72

♠ AKQ983
♥ AQ
♦ 752
♣ Q4

N	E	S	W
–	NB	1S	2C
Dbl*	NB	3S	NB
4S			

North's first bid is a Negative Double, indicating a four-card heart suit
with 8pts or more (or possibly a five-card heart suit with 6/7pts).

West leads A♣ and is encouraged by East with 7♣. West continues
with K♣ and, on the third round, West plays 5♣. East trumps with 10♠
and if declarer over-trumps with Q♠, this promotes West's J♠ into a
natural trick. Since South will also lose the heart finesse, this means
that declarer will be down.

To protect her trump holding, therefore, South should not over-
ruff East's 10♠, but instead discard Q♥. Whatever East plays now,
declarer can draw trumps and claim the rest.

Notice that West led 5♣ at trick three. Holding ♠J74, she wanted
East to ruff this trick and tempt South to over-ruff. Although East
should work out from the bidding that both she and declarer are now
void, West should make it easy for her partner. If West leads J♣, a
careless (or over-thinking) East might decline to ruff, and now the
defence is dead.

The Scissors Coup

A 'coup' sounds a very elitist, expert play to make but, as you improve, and begin to foresee what might happen later in the hand, a Scissors Coup is very much achievable and, as you will see, highly desirable.

Dealer North
Game All

```
                        ♠ J965
                        ♥ A10
                        ♦ J7
                        ♣ KQJ83

    ♠ 73                  N           ♠ A8
    ♥ 5432          W         E       ♥ QJ87
    ♦ Q92                 S           ♦ AK8653
    ♣ 9765                            ♣ 4

                        ♠ KQ1042
                        ♥ K96
                        ♦ 104
                        ♣ A102
```

N	E	S	W
1C	1D	1S	NB
2S	DBl	**4S**	

West leads 2♦ to East's K♦ and East switches to 4♣. This is clearly a singleton, so declarer must now think about what might happen if she takes the standard line of pulling trumps immediately. Most likely East will win and return a low diamond to West's Q♦ (West's opening lead of 2♦ suggesting an honour). West will then lead a club for East to ruff, and the contract will be defeated.

To prevent this defence, declarer must seek to cut communications between the opponents' hands and, in particular, to prevent East from putting West on lead with a diamond. To this end, before drawing trumps, South should play A♥, K♥ and a third heart. When West follows low, declarer now throws J♦ from the table. East wins but now, crucially, cannot put West on lead to provide the killing club ruff.

This is what good bridge is about. Drawing inferences from your opponent or opponents' actions, forming an idea of what they are trying to do, learn from that, and then seek to counter it. This is why bridge is very much the thinking woman's pastime!

Dealer East
N/S Game

```
                          ♠ Q8732
                          ♥ 763
                          ♦ KQ
                          ♣ 543
    ♠ KJ105                                      ♠ 964
    ♥ 42               ┌─────────┐               ♥ KQJ1085
    ♦ J1074            │    N    │               ♦ 9653
    ♣ A106             │  W   E  │               ♣ –
                       │    S    │
                       └─────────┘
                          ♠ A
                          ♥ A9
                          ♦ A82
                          ♣ KQJ9872
```

N	E	S	W
–	2H*	4C	NB
5C			

East's Weak 2H opener seems standard, but, at favourable vulnerability, it is the expert style these days to pre-empt at the three-level on a six-card suit, providing the texture is good. Certainly East's hand is useless in defence, so such an aggressive action would be justified.

South might have punted 3NT. If partner has A♣, the contract should be cold; if partner does not hold A♣, one hold-up in hearts may leave East unable to regain the lead.

West leads 4♥ to East's 10♥. If South is confident that East will always have exactly six hearts for her bid, she might duck this lead, but when she sees 4♥ she worries that West may hold a singleton and so she wins the trick.

If, at trick two, declarer leads trumps, West will take A♣ immediately and play 2♥. East will win and lead a third heart. Now, if declarer trumps low, West over-ruffs with 10♣; if declarer trumps high, West discards another suit and waits to take her 10♣, which has now been promoted by South having to trump high. This is the setting trick.

South should pause at trick one and reflect that the one possible defence to beat her would be if West holds all three trumps and East can get in to lead hearts, forming just such a trump promotion. To guard against this possibility, before drawing trumps, South should cash A♠, cross to dummy with Q♦ and lead Q♠. As expected, East does not hold K♠ and follows low, so South can throw 9♥ from hand. West wins, but now when she leads her remaining heart, South trumps, so West ends up making only one natural trump trick.

This final hand is a loser-exchange of the purest kind, leading to a Scissors Coup.

Dealer East
E/W Game

```
                          ♠ J4
                          ♥ A87
                          ♦ J54
                          ♣ KJ1093
        ♠ K762                              ♠ AQ983
        ♥ 5              ┌─────────┐        ♥ K62
        ♦ 8762          │    N    │        ♦ K1093
        ♣ 7654          │  W   E  │        ♣ 8
                         │    S    │
                         └─────────┘
                          ♠ 105
                          ♥ QJ10943
                          ♦ AQ
                          ♣ AQ2
```

N	E	S	W
–	1S	2H	2S
3C	3S	**4H**	

North's 3C is a Fit non-jump (page 154). If E/W had not been vulnerable, West would bid on to 4S as a sacrifice.

West leads 2♠ to East's A♠ and East switches to 8♣. This is clearly a singleton and declarer should appreciate that West's 2♠ indicates an honour with which East can put West on lead to provide the club ruff.

Declarer considers her options. Playing A♥ and another might work but, here, with East holding three trumps, it does not. Instead, using the auction as a guide, declarer should win the club switch in dummy, but playing Q♣ from hand to unblock the suit. Then, she takes the diamond finesse. When that wins, she can cash A♦, play a heart to A♥ and lead J♦. When East covers with K♦, declarer discards her remaining spade, and West can never be put on lead again.

2

DEFENCE

I want to urge you, as strongly as I can, to do two things.

If you find these hands hard to visualise, lay them out on a table at home with real playing cards and observe the action. It really is worth the effort.

Take more time when defending.

While the declarer is studying dummy, recall the auction, add up the points on the hand and assess how many your partner is likely to hold; ask yourself what partner's lead means, count the tricks you think the declarer may have, or that your side may be able to make. Use the time to immerse yourself in this world of fifty-two cards and seek ways to achieve your goals.

Even if declarer plays immediately from dummy (a sure sign of a weak player), just refuse to play to the first trick. You can say, out loud: 'That's too quick for me. I have to think about the hand.' And then sit there and think. It really will help enormously. And, as you force yourself to do this, it will become easier, and the revelations you begin to experience will transform your game and make you feel in greater control, increasingly confident, and relishing more the prospect of defending a contract.

Defence should be the time when your partnership is most as one. Successful defences will lead to a warm, fuzzy feeling verging on love for your partner, whereas missed opportunities will soon result in acrimony and discord. For this reason, when playing with your regular partner, or group of friends, it is best to settle upon a simple, workable defensive strategy which will prove powerful and successful most of the time.

Defensive System

Opening lead, signal, and discard style

Opening leads against suit contracts:
- Fourth highest from an honour, or honours, not including a ten on its own.
- Top-of-rubbish, or second top from a suit headed by a ten, from suits without an honour at the head of the suit.
- Top of touching honours; occasionally just two honours; more desirably from three honours, or broken sequence; internal sequence, *not* from suits headed by the ace.
- From AK, lead of the ace asks partner for Attitude signal; lead of the king asks partner for Count Signal;
- Reluctance to lead doubletons unless partner has called the suit, or you hold a weak hand.
- Trump leads from two- and three-card holdings.

KQJxx **K**Q10xx **K**Qxx **9**742 10**8**643 K**J**104

Opening leads against NT contracts:
- Fourth highest from an honour, or honours, not including a ten on its own.
- Top-of-rubbish, or second top from a suit headed by a ten, or from suits without an honour at the head of the suit.
- Top of three touching honours; broken sequence; internal sequence.
- Lead of ace from AKx.

KQJxx **K**Q10xx KQ**xx** **9**742 10**8**643 K**J**104 A**J**1084

Signals and discards against suit contracts:
- Attitude (High = encouraging; low = discouraging) when partner leads an ace, or when partner leads and the second hand to play plays ace.

- Count (high = even number of cards held; low = odd number of cards held), when partner leads any card bar the ace (unless the ace is played immediately by an opponent) and whenever an opponent leads a suit.

  NB: in this context, an odd number is *very* often three.

- Suit-Preference (McKenney) Discards. Your first discard indicates disinterest in the suit played, with interest shown in the higher or lower remaining suits (excluding trumps) by the size of the card discarded. This is indicative of where your strength lies, *not* a demand for partner to lead the suit. Use the highest card you can afford to signal with, or your very lowest card – be clear.

Signals and discards against NT contracts:
- All as above, plus:
- when partner leads an honour card, almost always overtake or jettison with any honour held in your hand. Exceptions are when by doing so you establish a trick in dummy for declarer, or you believe you have the longer holding in the suit.

Leading to partner's called suit:
- Usually as above; higher card from a doubleton. Occasionally, top of partner's called suit, depending upon where your opponents' strength is located. With strength to your left and weakness to your right, a high card usually works best.
- Top-of-rubbish from three small cards (opposed to MUD). This leaves declarer (and sometimes partner) guessing whether you hold two or three cards. This can be advantageous.

As we look at further elements, we will see examples of these techniques in action, plus further description.

Some players favour 'Reverse Count' and 'Reverse Attitude', reversing the meaning of the high and low cards. There is a small advantage to this technique, but unless you play it consistently, the opportunity for errors may outweigh the benefits.

Overtake and jettison

While there are some drawbacks to this agreement, the advantages far outweigh them.

When partner leads an honour card against a NT contract, you are required to overtake with a higher honour, and return the lead, or jettison (throw away) a lower honour card, to reveal their position, unblock, and clarify the layout. Failure to jettison or unblock therefore denies an honour, allowing partner to place these cards in the declarer's hand.

With no honours to jettison or unblock, show count (the number of cards held in the suit: high card = equal number; low = odd number).

West		East
♠ 764	N / W E / S	♠ 985
♥ KQ1085		♥ J32
♦ 983		♦ QJ5
♣ A2		♣ J985

With South in 3NT, West leads K♥, East immediately discards J♥. West continues to play top hearts until A♥ is pushed out, and regains the lead with A♣ to defeat the contract.

Dealer South
Game All

	♠ Q964	
	♥ 75	
	♦ AK6	
	♣ KJ64	

♠ 853	N / W E / S	♠ A107
♥ KQ1093		♥ 862
♦ 952		♦ 10743
♣ A10		♣ 752

	♠ KJ2	
	♥ AJ4	
	♦ QJ8	
	♣ Q983	

N	E	S	W
–	–	1NT	NB
2C*	NB	2D	NB
3NT			

Following a Stayman enquiry, North bids the standard 3NT. West leads K♥. Dummy, partner and declarer all play low.

West knows that East does not hold either A♥ or J♥, so these can be placed in the South hand, who is forming the 'Bath Coup' – by ducking, South has made it impossible for West to lead the suit again without giving South two quick tricks. East's 2♥ is a Count Signal indicating an odd number of cards (very often three). West switches to 8♠ (top-of-rubbish) seeking an entry to East's hand. East wins with A♠ and returns 8♥, breaking open the heart suit so that, when West wins A♣, she has heart winners to cash.

These are two very standard examples of the defensive agreement in action.

What's happening here?

Dealer South
Game All

```
            ♠ AJ64
            ♥ A75
            ♦ J64
            ♣ K83
♠ 853
♥ 986          N        West leads K♦
♦ KQ1053    W     E     East plays 8♦
♣ A10          S
```

N	E	S	W
–	–	1NT	NB
3NT			

West leads K♦, dummy plays low; East plays 8♦, declarer plays 2♦.

West must consider the meaning of this first trick. East appears to be denying A♦, but – crucially – if East does hold A♦ and overtakes K♦, then returns the suit, this would set up dummy's J♦ as a trick. Additionally, if declarer had held A♦, she would win the trick immediately, knowing that dummy's J♦ would be a second stopper later. It would make no sense for the declarer to duck and possibly forfeit a trick. For that reason, at trick two, West must lead a low diamond to partner's A♦. This was the full deal:

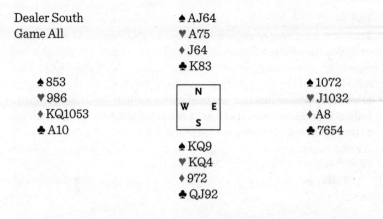

Dealer South
Game All

	♠ AJ64	
	♥ A75	
	♦ J64	
	♣ K83	
♠ 853		♠ 1072
♥ 986		♥ J1032
♦ KQ1053		♦ A8
♣ A10		♣ 7654
	♠ KQ9	
	♥ KQ4	
	♦ 972	
	♣ QJ92	

The one other time when you might not overtake or jettison is when you suspect that you hold more cards in the suit than your partner. This may occur when holding four cards, but more likely it is if you are holding five cards in the suit your partner has led. Then, hoping that your partner has led from a two- or three-card suit, trying to find your long suit, you simply make a Count Signal.

One simple last point, inserted here because I am asked so very often about it.

Against a NT contract, partner leads the king and you hold both the ace and jack.

You overtake with the ace, and return the jack. This both fulfils your need to indicate where the honours lie, and unblocks the suit.

Peculiar NT leads

There are a handful of strange leads against NT contracts which give your side the best chance of taking tricks.

AKJ64

From this holding, the correct lead in our system would be the king. This is because we want partner to show us count or, in the unlikely event that she holds the queen, to jettison it.

```
                        ♣ 1083
   ♣ AKJ64                                        ♣ 752
                        ♣ Q9
```

West leads K♣, dummy shows three clubs headed by the ten, East plays 2♣. This denies Q♣ and shows either a singleton, giving South four clubs, or three cards, leaving declarer with just ♣Q9. If South holds four clubs, the defence is probably dead, so West should continue with A♣, felling declarer's Q♣ and taking the first five tricks.

```
                        ♣ 1083
   ♣ AKJ64                                        ♣ 72
                        ♣ Q95
```

West leads K♣, dummy shows three to the ten, East plays 7♣. East is denying Q♣. 7♣ seems high (2♣ has not appeared), so East is showing two cards in clubs (if she held four, this would leave South with only one). So, unless West holds a certain re-entry, she does not continue clubs but attempts to find an entry to the East hand, so that East can return a club through South's Q♣ and West can then win all her club tricks.

AK5

From this holding, the correct lead is the ace, asking partner to encourage with length in the suit, or discourage with shortage. This can be a very powerful option.

```
                        ♣ 983
   ♣ AK5                                          ♣ 107642
                        ♣ QJ
```

West leads A♣, dummy lays down ♣983. East counts three clubs in West's hand, three in dummy, five in her hand, leaving South with a doubleton. This means that, on the third round, East's 10♣ will be good. East therefore encourages with 7♣ – the highest card she can afford. West should read this as high (she cannot see 6♣, 4♣ or 2♣ on the first trick) and cash K♣ and lead 5♣. East-West duly take the first five tricks.

Similarly with:

Dealer South		♠ A4	
Game All		♥ Q96	
		♦ KJ1096	
		♣ K83	

♠ 108653		♠ J72
♥ AK5	N	♥ 8432
♦ 42	W E	♦ AQ8
♣ 1074	S	♣ 952

		♠ KQ9	
		♥ J107	
		♦ 753	
		♣ AQJ6	

N	E	S	W
–	–	1NT	NB
3NT			

West does not make a speculative spade lead, but prefers to try A♥ to look at dummy and see partner's reaction. Although East holds only four hearts, she works out that as South and dummy both hold three hearts, her fourth heart will become a winner. With her commanding holding in dummy's long suit, East counts five almost certain defensive tricks: three hearts and two diamonds. She wants to make it clear to West: she drops 8♥ at trick one. West continues with K♥ and 5♥ and East later makes ♦AQ and 4♥ before declarer has nine tricks.

AQ1064

Against a NT contract, from any holding containing three honours (a ten is an honour when it is with other honours; it is not counted as an honour when alone), it is almost always correct to lead an honour but, here, you have no sequence of any kind. To attempt to smother a singleton or doubleton jack, you should lead one of your top honours.

- If you have a certain outside entry, start with the ace. Partner will have to work out that this is unlikely to be from AKx, and signal accordingly.
- If you have no outside entry, lead the queen, preserving the ace as your re-entry. Partner will overtake or jettison with an honour, or show count with no honours.

♣ J7

♣ AQ1053   ♣ 642

♣ K98

If West leads A♣ (suggesting that she has a certain re-entry to her hand), East will play 2♣, denying an honour and indicating a one- or three-card holding. West can continue with Q♣, smothering dummy's J♣, and continue with a third round of clubs to clear the suit.

If West leads Q♣ (suggesting that she has no re-entry to her hand outside of clubs), East will play 2♣, denying an honour and indicating a one- or three-card holding. West can now continue with a low club, establishing the suit for her side and leaving East with a club in her hand to lead when she, hopefully, gains the lead.

These three unusual lead styles are very important and can result in some excellent scores when playing against less experienced partnerships or players.

Trick Development

Many defensive techniques require you to imagine what cards your partner might hold. Take your time when dummy first hits the table, so that you can consider what action may need to be taken.

Setting up extra tricks quickly

When the dummy is balanced, there is generally no hurry to set up tricks quickly: you can sit back and wait for your high cards to pull their weight. However, if dummy contains a long side-suit, this can be used by the declarer to discard losers in another suit from her hand and, in that situation, you do have to act quickly to take your tricks. Here, East is on lead after dummy has gone down, with no other high cards in hand. Although leading away from an ace is considered a heinous crime, there are times when it may be right – just almost never as an opening lead.

♠ KQ9

♠ J752 ♠ A104

♠ 863

If her partner holds J♠, her side will make two spade tricks *given time*. However, if speed is required, East should lead 4♠. This will run to West's J♠ and dummy will win. When West regains the lead, a second spade now allows East to take both A♠ and 10♠.

Notice that, even if South holds J♠, this defence is unlikely to cost a trick. Ultimately, leading away from an ace is acceptable if you can still take a king or queen with that card subsequently.

Forcing declarer's (or dummy's) high card into a trick

It is rarely correct to lead the highest card in a suit unless you have touching cards but, again, when you must take several tricks quickly, it has to be considered.

♠ 732

```
   N
W     E
   S
```

♠ AJ104

♠ Q65

♠ K98

East is on lead, with no other high cards. Her side must take tricks now, before South can cash her own winners. To succeed, West must hold ♠AJ10 or ♠AJx (with declarer mistakenly failing to cover the first lead).

If East leads a standard low spade, South can cover with 9♠ and West wins with 10♠. However, now West cannot lead another spade without setting up South's K♠. To avoid this, to cash tricks quickly and when you hold no re-entry, East must lead her highest card to push declarer's presumed K♠ into West's winning tenace (AJ10). Here, Q♠ consigns South to losing all three tricks – fast!

Surround plays

These plays remove declarer's winning option from certain card combinations. You will require imagination and judgement to decide when this play will benefit you. In these two prime examples, you will see that your attention must be on the pips in your hand, relative to those to your right. This is why, in defence, it is generally easier for the hand with dummy on her right than for the hand with declarer on her right.

♠ 1052

```
   N
W     E
   S
```

♠ A87

♠ KJ94

♠ Q63

E/W must make spade tricks quickly. If East leads the standard 4♠, South should play low, allowing dummy's ten to force West to play her ace. As a result, South's Q♠ wins the third round.

However, if East leads J♠, her ♠K9 still *surround* dummy's ♠105, and it means that South must play Q♠ or allow East's jack to hold the trick. In this way, E/W score all the spade tricks.

How does East know the layout of the suit? She may well not but, if her side are to take three quick spade tricks, West must hold A♠ and, on that basis, if South holds Q♠, only J♠ will work. By the way, if West holds both A♠ and Q♠, the lead of J♠ does not cost, nor does it cost if South holds A♠ and West holds Q♠.

♠ 962

♠ K753

	N	
W		E
	S	

♠ Q108

♠ AJ4

East is on lead, trying to establish two spade tricks. If East leads 8♠, South will duck, and dummy's 9♠ will force West to take her K♠. East's Q♠ will now be finessed by South's ♠AJ. However, if East leads 10♠, South's J♠ must be played to avoid 10♠ from winning, and East's ♠Q8 still *surrounds* dummy's ♠96.

Again, it is very unlikely that East's play of 10♠ can cost. She needs West to hold at least K♠ and, if she does, the play of 10♠ ensures maximum trick-taking potential.

Dealer North   ♠ J1042
Love All   ♥ 1054
                  ♦ A1096
                  ♣ 85

♠ Q9753   ♠ 86
♥ K32   N   ♥ AJ96
♦ Q743   W   E   ♦ J52
♣ 9   S   ♣ Q1063

                  ♠ AK
                  ♥ Q87
                  ♦ K8
                  ♣ AKJ742

N	E	S	W
–	–	1C	NB
1S	NB	**3NT**	

West leads 5♠ against South's 3NT. Declarer wins perforce, goes to dummy with A♦ and takes the club finesse. Even though J♣ holds, because of the 4-1 break, when South continues cashing top clubs, East scores her Q♣ on the fourth round. East realises that with a total of five club tricks now makeable for South, surely her side must take four tricks immediately, or concede defeat. If West holds K♥ and South Q♥ is there any way to score all four hearts tricks quickly? Crucially, East's ♥J9 surround dummy's 10♥, and East also holds A♥. This is the perfect time to trap South's Q♥ in a Surround Play. East duly leads J♥ and now, whatever declarer does, E/W must score all four heart tricks to defeat the contract.

The next hand was defended by two online bridge robots (yes, really!): and they made very fine use of this play:

Dealer North
Love All

	♠ Q103	
	♥ K763	
	♦ Q62	
	♣ K62	

♠ J9862		♠ 754
♥ J85	**N**	♥ Q94
♦ AJ8	**W E**	♦ K974
♣ A4	**S**	♣ 953

	♠ AK	
	♥ A102	
	♦ 1053	
	♣ QJ1087	

N	**E**	**S**	**W**
NB	NB	1C	NB
1H	NB	**1NT**	

South's 1NT rebid here indicated 12–14pts and really South's hand is worth at least 15pts in no-trumps. However, it was as well that South underbid, since things did not go well …

West led 6♠ to East's 4♠ and declarer's K♠. South led 7♣ and West hopped in with A♣, before switching instantly to J♦. Not only was West employing a Surround Play, but the robot was also doing so from the shorter holding, hoping that East held four or more diamonds. From the bidding (where South had opened a better minor), this was very reasonable.

The J♦ lead surrounds not only dummy's Q♦, but also declarer's 10♦. Dummy covered J♦ with Q♦ and East won with K♦ and returned 7♦. Declarer might have achieved a block by playing low, but covered instead with 10♦ and the defence took all four diamond tricks.

It's a bit worrying that computers are making these perfect plays instantly … I want an opponent to struggle and sweat just a little before making a killing play against me. Psychologically, this is bad news for us human thinkers …

Surround plays are just the best way to handle a suit and, as such, are available to both the declarer and the defenders. Because the declarer can see her partner's hand, we routinely make these plays without much thought. It is the imagining of the layout which is required for defenders, and this is why it is that much harder to produce these plays as a defender.

Keeping Secrets

Any decent declarer will use information from the auction, the opening lead and subsequent plays to place the missing cards in her opponents' hands. As a defender, your job is to keep your partner well informed, while keeping the declarer – as far as you can – in the dark.

Not winning finesses

For this first technique, imagine yourself as the declarer and remember how much relief you feel when a vital finesse works. Often, it blinds the declarer to any other line of play which is why, when the finesse is actually wrong, you want to make the declarer believe that it is, actually, right.

Dealer North
Love All

```
                    ♠ A
                    ♥ 862
                    ♦ AKJ63
                    ♣ J863
   ♠ 75432                        ♠ 10986
   ♥ A3          N                ♥ J75
   ♦ 874      W     E             ♦ 95
   ♣ AK4          S               ♣ Q1095
                    ♠ KQJ
                    ♥ KQ1094
                    ♦ Q102
                    ♣ 72
```

N	E	S	W
1D	NB	1H	NB
2H	NB	**4H**	

West leads A♣ and, duly encouraged, continues with K♣ and 4♣, South ruffing the third round. Declarer crosses to A♠ and leads a heart to her king. West wins, and gets off lead. Declarer wins in hand, crosses to A♦ and leads a heart to finesse East for J♥. Contract made.

This is how the hand plays out among kitchen bridge players and, all too often, among club players also. Simply, West has revealed the position of A♥, making the declarer's life easy.

When declarer leads a heart to her king, if West plays 3♥ smoothly, South will place the A♥ with East. She will cross to dummy with a top diamond and lead a second heart. When East follows low, South will almost certainly play Q♥ from hand. West wins, and East scores her J♥ later to defeat the contract.

In no-trumps especially, a finesse which will be repeated by the declarer should usually not be won by the defender the first time.

Dealer North
Love All

		♠ 73
		♥ A53
		♦ 82
		♣ KJ8742

♠ AQ			♠ 86542
♥ 109862	N		♥ Q4
♦ 543	W E		♦ J1097
♣ A53	S		♣ Q6

		♠ KJ109
		♥ KJ7
		♦ AKQ6
		♣ 109

N	E	S	W
NB	NB	1D	NB
2C	NB	**3NT**	

West leads 10♥ and, the moment dummy hits baize, East should be thinking along these lines: dummy is very minimum for her 2C response, so the contract will rest on the long club suit. With only one outside entry to the table, if West holds A♣, we can cut declarer off from the clubs. If the declarer finesses with J♣, I am going to risk playing low.

East must prepare for this play well before it happens. It is not difficult to foresee that the declarer's first move is likely to be establishing clubs. Even if East has to keep declarer waiting at trick 1, she should do so. This is the key time for both declarer and defenders to make decisions about their lines of play.

In simple terms if, when South leads 10♣ and finesses, East wins with Q♣, declarer will prevail. On the other hand, if East ducks the first club trick smoothly, West will place Q♣ in the West hand. She will repeat the finesse, overtaking 9♣ with J♣. This time, East wins, and because West still holds A♣, declarer cannot get to dummy to dislodge A♣ and then get there a second time to enjoy the club winners.

Next, very satisfyingly, let's suggest to the declarer that the losing finesse is actually right, and in doing so making the winning finesse seem wrong. That is a mouthful, but you'll see what I mean . . .

Dealer North
Love All

			♠ AK4	
			♥ 832	
			♦ 764	
			♣ 9532	

♠ QJ1032				♠ 76
♥ 764		N		♥ QJ109
♦ K92	W		E	♦ 853
♣ J8		S		♣ K1064

			♠ 985	
			♥ AK5	
			♦ AQJ10	
			♣ AQ7	

N	E	S	W
NB	NB	1D	NB
2C	NB	**3NT**	

West leads Q♠ and declarer wins in dummy with K♠, and plays 4♦. East follows low, South puts in J♦ and West wins with K♦. When declarer is next in dummy, she will now take the club finesse, which is correct, and nine tricks will be made.

As you already know by now, West should not have won that first diamond finesse. If West follows with 2♦, and looks her usual morose self, declarer will place K♦ in the East hand. When she returns to dummy with A♠, she will use the entry to take the 'winning' diamond finesse – except, this time, West does win K♦ and continues spades, and South never gets the chance to take the club finesse, which was right all along.

So simple; so beautiful.

Playing the card you are known to hold

This is so simple, yet relentlessly ignored by most bridge players. Get it right and you will certainly outwit good players – because bridge players who know a tiny bit more than others usually assume that everyone else at the table knows nothing about the game whatsoever, they simply won't expect you to be up to it.

♠ KJ3

	N	
W		E
	S	

♠ Q105 ♠ 762

♠ A984

South leads 4♠, West plays 5♠, J♠ is chosen from the dummy, and this wins. Declarer cashes dummy's K♠: East plays low, declarer plays low, West plays 10♠. Declarer leads 3♠ from dummy, East plays low and, knowing that West holds Q♠, declarer plays A♠, felling West's queen. Now, 9♠ is a fourth winner in hand.

Simply, when the first finesse won, everyone knew that West held Q♠. But no one knows who holds 10♠. Once J♠ has been played, Q♠ and 10♠ have the same value. So, on the second trick, West must drop Q♠ – *the card she is known to hold*. Now, when declarer leads 3♠ from dummy and East plays low, South will almost always insert 9♠ to finesse against East for 10♠. West will win, and at least one trick has been saved.

Not to play Q♠ here is just plain lazy. If this doesn't hit you as completely obvious, please lay a suit out on the table and practise this. Once you have it, it is easy and you will never forget it.

This is a tiny manoeuvre, but it can make a huge difference.

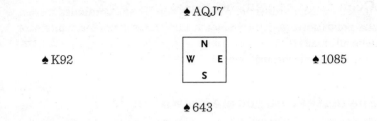

♠ AQJ7

♠ K92

N
W　E
S

♠ 1085

♠ 643

Declarer leads a low spade from hand, West plays low and J♠ is selected from dummy. This holds the trick. Declarer returns to hand and leads another spade. It cannot cost for you to play the card you are known to hold – the K♠ – here. By doing so, declarer may place East with ♠10985 and give up on cashing A♠ until later, hunting for an extra trick(s) elsewhere. If West plays low, declarer wins Q♠ and finds that it is safe to cash A♠ to test for the 3-3 break and, when she does, the extra trick is made without so much as a drop of perspiration forming on her brow.

Incidentally, withholding information about cards held is also a vital technique for declarer. Take this simple example. South is in a 3NT contract and West leads J♠.

♠ 953

♠ J7

N
W　E
S

♠ A8642

♠ KQ10

West leads J♠ from ♠J7, trying to find East's long suit. She succeeds and, when East decides to win, declarer drops 10♠ from hand.

From the lead, East knows that South holds Q♠ and, since West has led a short suit, South almost certainly holds K♠ too. East can work out that the spade suit is dead and switch to something, quite probably, more lethal.

All South needs to do is to drop the card she is known to hold: Q♠. Now, East will wonder if declarer didn't start with ♠KQ and West with ♠J107, and East will probably return a spade, which is unlikely to trouble South.

Occluding the count

This is a beautiful hand in which a defender identified a situation where to make the normal play would give the declarer only a winning option. The play failed, however – as brilliant plays sometimes do – because this declarer wasn't really watching anything, let alone thinking about what she might have seen.

Dealer West
Game All

```
                        ♠ 653
                        ♥ A103
                        ♦ AKQ7
                        ♣ 1084
        ♠ KJ                              ♠ 102
        ♥ KQJ875            N             ♥ 964
        ♦ J1042         W       E         ♦ 953
        ♣ 3                S              ♣ AK652
                        ♠ AQ9874
                        ♥ 2
                        ♦ 86
                        ♣ QJ97
```

N	E	S	W
–	–	–	1H
NB	2H	2S	3H
4S			

West, thinking it unlikely that her side would make a heart trick, led 3♣. East won K♣, cashed A♣ and led a third round of clubs. West realised, now that East had shown up with 7pts, that her own hand would be counted for all the remaining values, including K♠. If she trumped the third round of clubs with J♠, declarer would subsequently lay down A♠ in a successful attempt to fell his now singleton K♠. With this in mind, West casually trumped the third club with K♠ – the card he **should** *be known to hold*. This is a fine play since declarer will now surely mark him with a singleton king and East with ♠J102. The correct play for South when tackling trumps would be to cross to dummy, lead a spade and, when East played small, put in 7♠ from hand.

Declarer, who was clearly not counting anything, disappointed

West hugely when, instead of drawing the most logical conclusion about the trump position – one which 99 per cent of the time would be right – instead slapped A♠ on the table and did not even blink when West's J♠ fell.

Trick Counting in Defence

Just as a declarer counts tricks (or losers) to formulate her plan, so good defenders should do the same. With the advantage of having heard the auction, seen dummy and witnessed partner's cards to early tricks, a defender should be able to count either her side's potential tricks, or those of the declarer.

Counting for tempo

How quickly and aggressively you defend will be influenced by how many tricks you believe the declarer is looking at. Compare these two problems:

1)
Dealer North
Love All

                          ♠ K432
                          ♥ AKQ
                          ♦ 105
                          ♣ J1063

♠ QJ1097
♥ 92
♦ AJ93
♣ K5

N	E	S	W
–	–	1NT	NB
2C*	NB	2D*	NB
3NT			

West leads Q♠, dummy plays K♠, partner plays 6♠, declarer plays 5♠. Declarer leads J♣ from dummy, partner plays 2♣, declarer 7♣ and West wins with K♣.

    Should West lead another top spade, or should she switch to a low diamond?

    West must count South's tricks: she has ♠AK, ♥AKQ (but the

Stayman bid confirms that she does not have a fourth heart in hand), and she has three club tricks. You know this last piece of information from East's 2♣ on the first round of clubs – a low card indicating, usually, a three-card holding. This marks South with four clubs, of which she can now only make three tricks.

Therefore, South only has eight tricks and, providing West does continue leading spades, a ninth cannot be found before West takes her A♦ and cashes three spade winners.

Here is the full deal.

Dealer North   ♠ K432
Love All   ♥ AKQ
                           ♦ 105
                           ♣ J1063

♠ QJ1097		♠ 6
♥ 92	N	♥ 107543
♦ AJ93	W E	♦ Q842
♣ K5	S	♣ 942

                           ♠ A85
                           ♥ J86
                           ♦ K76
                           ♣ AQ87

By continuing with spades, West forces declarer to rely on East holding A♦. When West wins, South loses the remaining spades to fail by one trick.

2)
Dealer East   ♠ 64
Love All   ♥ AK3
                           ♦ 74
                           ♣ KQJ1074

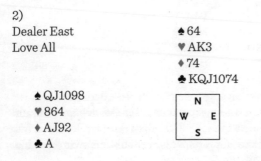

♠ QJ1098	
♥ 864	N
♦ AJ92	W E
♣ A	S

N	E	S	W
NB	NB	1NT	NB
3NT			

West leads Q♠, dummy plays low, East plays 5♠, declarer wins with K♠.

    South leads a club and West wins perforce.

    Should West continue spades or switch to a diamond?

    West counts declarer's tricks: two spades (East cannot hold A♠), ♥AK, and five club tricks. That makes nine tricks. To defeat the contract, East-West must take four tricks right now. The count of points on the hand allows for East to hold K♦, so West switches to 2♦. East wins with K♦ and returns 8♦, to declarer's 10♦ and West's J♦. A♦ is cashed and South's Q♦ falls, so West cashes her fourth diamond to defeat the contract.

    Here is the whole hand.

Dealer East
Love All

    ♠ 64
    ♥ AK3
    ♦ 74
    ♣ KQJ1074

♠ QJ1098
♥ 864
♦ AJ92
♣ A

    ♠ 53
    ♥ 10975
    ♦ K865
    ♣ 652

    ♠ AK72
    ♥ QJ2
    ♦ Q103
    ♣ 983

N	E	S	W
NB	NB	1NT	NB
3NT			

At the table, East won K♦ and returned 8♦. Some players might win and return 5♦ – the normal card – but when dummy contains low cards, it is often better to play a card higher than those on the table. Whichever East opts for, the defence will prevail.

    At Duplicate Pairs, the lead of 2♦ from West risks giving N/S an overtrick if East holds Q♦ and South K♦. Generally, in club duplicates, do not worry about these overtricks as a defender – focus on beating the contract if it is a realistic proposition.

Foreseeing the setting trick

If your target to beat the contract is four tricks, there is little point in making a plan to take three. Yet laziness often leaves us doing exactly that.

Dealer North
Love All

	♠ K1095	
	♥ Q10	
	♦ KQ1076	
	♣ AK	

♠ 63		♠ A82
♥ KJ432	N	♥ 965
♦ 4	W E	♦ A953
♣ Q8732	S	♣ 1095

	♠ QJ74	
	♥ A87	
	♦ J82	
	♣ J64	

N	E	S	W
1D	NB	1S	NB
4S			

Even seeing all four hands, the defence may not be immediately recognisable. West leads 4♦ and East can win and return a diamond for a ruff. East makes A♠ later, but that is all the defence come to, since South will use dummy's long diamonds to discard two hearts from hand.

When East sees the lead, this is what she should think: A♦, a diamond ruff and A♠ are three tricks; from where might a fourth come? Partner has no more than two trumps, so a second ruff is impossible. If partner has A♥, the fourth trick is easy, but if partner holds K♥ then East must lead a heart through the declarer's hand to establish it – West cannot profitably lead from K♥ herself.

So, having won A♦, East does *not* provide a diamond ruff, but instead switches to 9♥. Whether South rises with A♥ or not, West's K♥ will make a trick immediately or subsequently. When declarer leads trumps, East rises with A♠, returns a diamond for the ruff and, if it has not already been made, West cashes K♥. Four tricks, and the contract is defeated.

You might argue that West could have only one trump and so delaying the ruff could be costly. However, it is unlikely that West has a singleton diamond and a singleton spade – to lead a singleton in a side-suit with only one trump is not recommended. This plan is certainly the best there is.

Here is another example of working out what the setting trick might be, and playing for that chance.

Dealer South	♠ 4	
Love All	♥ 532	
	♦ AQJ1087	
	♣ KJ3	

♠ J109852		♠ KQ3
♥ Q86	N W E S	♥ A74
♦ 9		♦ 6432
♣ 954		♣ A76

	♠ A76	
	♥ KJ109	
	♦ K5	
	♣ Q1082	

N	E	S	W
–	–	1NT	NB
3NT			

West leads J♠; East should assess that West holds between 2 and 4pts. East overtakes J♠ with Q♠, and South ducks. East lays down K♠ and South ducks again. What should East do now?

If East plays a third spade, South will win, cash diamond tricks sooner or later, and then push out A♣. East has no further spades to lead and the defence will be dead. East must be pragmatic: after the second round, the spade defence is dead. What cards could West hold to defeat the contract?

If West holds Q♣ or K♦ they are useless, as is J♥. If West holds K♥, all is easy. If West holds Q♥, then it is essential that East leads one now. At trick three, East leads 4♥ and, whether South guesses correctly or not, this sets up Q♥ to be a trick either immediately or later. When East wins A♣, E/W will come to two spades, two hearts and A♣ to beat the contract.

Anticipating declarer's plan

There is an old bridge saying that you can never play more than 25 per cent better than the worst player at your table, and it may be true. Certainly, when you play at your club, you should seek out the best players and play against them as often as possible.

Most declarers would make the same plan on this hand, so can you find the correct defensive attack?

Dealer South   ♠ K10743
Love All   ♥ 52
                         ♦ 10874
                         ♣ Q4

	N	
W		E
	S	

                                ♠ QJ98
                                ♥ 63
                                ♦ QJ95
                                ♣ KJ10

N	E	S	W
–	–	1H	NB
1S	NB	**3H**	

West leads A♦ and down comes the expected awful dummy. South's bid suggests a six-card suit with 15–18pts, and probably six or seven tricks. K♠ looks like one, but where else might dummy provide a trick – and what can East do about it?

Neither dummy's spades nor diamonds seem capable of providing any extra tricks (other than K♠), so the one facet that South might try to put to good use is dummy's doubleton club. Perhaps West will work this out and switch to trumps but, possibly, West has a holding from which she does not want to lead a heart, something like ♥Qxx. It looks like East must do the work.

East should drop Q♦ under the ace – this promises either a singleton or J♦ and is a very useful play to indicate that you want the lead. West underleads her K♦, playing 3♦ to East's 9♦ or J♦ (depending on which card is played from dummy), and now East switches to a trump. South wins, leads a low club to Q♣ in dummy and East's K♣, and then East plays a second trump. This prevents the crucial club ruff in dummy and defeats the contract. Here's the full hand:

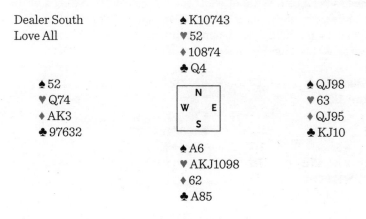

Dealer South
Love All

♠ K10743
♥ 52
♦ 10874
♣ Q4

♠ 52
♥ Q74
♦ AK3
♣ 97632

♠ QJ98
♥ 63
♦ QJ95
♣ KJ10

♠ A6
♥ AKJ1098
♦ 62
♣ A85

No other defence succeeds in taking five tricks.

Passivity

There are many times in defence, especially against NT contracts, when you must attack to gain a tempo, and establish your tricks before the declarer develops hers.

However, when defending suit contracts, it is often correct to utilise a very safe, passive defensive style, since any other option is likely to provide extra chances and tricks for the declarer. It is on these hands that I witness defenders making the most mistakes: sometimes, discipline really does pay dividends.

The need for passive defence

The most frequent situation for a passive defence is when the dummy hand is balanced. Without shortages for ruffing, or a long suit to establish, the declarer is often reliant upon finesses or on the defenders providing extra opportunities for her. Your job is to recognise this situation, and do precisely the opposite.

Dealer South
Love All

♠ KQJ2
♥ 85
♦ 74
♣ 108642

♠ 5
♥ AK43
♦ KJ53
♣ KJ97

```
      N
  W       E
      S
```

N	E	S	W
–	–	1S	Dbl
3S	NB	**4S**	

You lead A♥; East plays 9♥. What do you do next?

From the auction, you knew that dummy would be weak (jump-support after an opponent's take-out double is always weak), and so it is. Dummy's only long suit is clubs, and you have that suit well guarded. Declarer cannot discard any losers from her hand because there is nothing in dummy on which she can possibly throw them. East's 9♥ certainly looks encouraging and is likely to mean she holds Q♥, but there is no need to risk anything. Simply cash K♥ and get off lead with the one card that is completely safe – 5♠.

Here is the full deal.

Dealer South   ♠ KQJ2
Love All   ♥ 85
                        ♦ 74
                        ♣ 108642

♠ 5		♠ 64
♥ AK43	N	♥ Q9762
♦ KJ53	W E	♦ 10962
♣ KJ97	S	♣ 53

                  ♠ A109873
                  ♥ J10
                  ♦ AQ8
                  ♣ AQ

- When the dummy is balanced, take no risks: lead as safely as possible.
- Avoid leading from suits headed by single honours.
- Do not lead from an honour if you suspect / can see lower honours to your right.
- Do not lead dummy's longest suit.
- Do not lead a doubleton, unless your partner has called the suit, or you are very weak.
- Do: lead trumps; lead a suit to make declarer trump in her own hand; lead to solid holdings, such as AK or KQJ.

Here is a hand that I now set routinely for my students:

Dealer South   ♠ Q732
Love All   ♥ AQ5
                     ♦ J64
                     ♣ Q62

                                   ♠ 108
                                   ♥ J10632
          N   ♦ 82
    W   E   ♣ K974
          S

N	E	S	W
–	–	1S	NB
3S	NB	**4S**	

West leads A♦ and East encourages with 8♦. West plays K♦, East 2♦. West leads 7♦ and East ruffs – and that holds the trick. What should East do now?

When this hand first appeared in a club duplicate, every East must have made the wrong decision because the score-card indicated that everyone in 4S had made it. But 4S can only succeed if East does something reckless.

Dealer South   ♠ Q732
Love All   ♥ AQ5
                     ♦ J64
                     ♣ Q62

♠ J5   ♠ 108
♥ K98   ♥ J10632
♦ AK1073   N   ♦ 82
♣ 1085   W   E   ♣ K974
              S

                   ♠ AK964
                   ♥ 74
                   ♦ Q95
                   ♣ AJ3

This is how the play ran:

     West led ♦AK7, East ruffed and . . . switched to 4♣. This allowed the declarer to play low from hand, winning with Q♣ in dummy. Two rounds of trumps were followed by the successful heart finesse and then a club was played from dummy and, when East played low, J♣ was put on from the South hand, which held the trick 4S made.

First, East should note that the dummy is totally flat: this immediately suggests a super-safe defence (there is no opportunity for the declarer to ruff, or to set up a long suit for discards). Next, when West leads a third diamond, it should be 10♦. This is a Suit-Preference Signal for hearts but, more importantly, it says: do *not* lead a club. Finally, when East ruffs trick three, she should reflect that her side has got off to a great start, and no risk should be taken. By leading away from K♣ with Q♣ on her right, East was giving the queen a chance to win a trick when, since the king is sitting over it, in normal play it can never do.

Any passive exit is fine: a trump; a heart (the finesse will have to be taken through West anyway) – just not a dangerous club. Simply submit to South's line of play and don't offer any chance of assistance.

When South comes to play clubs herself, all East must do is save her K♣ for putting on top of dummy's Q♣ – South, now, cannot score more than two club tricks.

Forcing defence is both passive and aggressive

A forcing defence occurs when you force the hand that is long in trumps (usually, but not exclusively, the declarer's hand), to ruff, hence reducing the number of trumps available for drawing opponents' trumps and maintaining control of the hand.

Not only is this an attacking measure by the opposition, it is usually completely safe, since ruffing in the hand long in trumps rarely produces any extra tricks for the declarer.

Dealer East
N/S Game

♠ 8
♥ K742
♦ AK1032
♣ 853

```
N       E       S       W
–       NB      1H      NB
1S      NB      3H      NB
4H
```

West must lead against South's 4H contract.

Resist the temptation to lead the singleton spade. Looking for ruffs is only a good idea when you have a weak hand – so you hope that your partner will be strong and contain winners – and not the right tactic when you are strong and hold four half-decent trumps. In that situation, you want to lead your side's longest suit in an attempt to make the declarer trump in hand. Lead A♦.

Dealer East
N/S Game

♠ J7542
♥ 96
♦ 864
♣ AKJ

♠ 8
♥ K742
♦ AK1032
♣ 853

Dummy comes down, and partner encourages with 9♦. You continue with K♦ and declarer ruffs. She then crosses to dummy with A♣ and leads 9♥ on which your partner plays 8♥, declarer 3♥. What should West do?

Declarer started with six trumps and, after trumping, K♦ is down to five. If West can make the declarer trump in hand again, she will have the same number of trumps as West, and declarer cannot then draw all the trumps without leaving herself with none. To succeed in making South trump in hand, West must wait until the dummy is void in trumps, so West smoothly ducks 9♥ and waits for declarer to repeat the finesse. On this second round, West wins K♥ and leads a third diamond. South trumps but must either now draw the trumps and lose Q♣ later, or fail to draw trumps and find that her second top spade is ruffed.

Dealer East
N/S Game

	♠ J7542	
	♥ 96	
	♦ 864	
	♣ AKJ	
♠ 8		♠ Q10963
♥ K742	N	♥ 8
♦ AK1032	W E	♦ Q975
♣ 853	S	♣ Q72
	♠ AK	
	♥ AQJ1053	
	♦ J	
	♣ 10964	

At no time did West take any risks with her leads. Every one of them was completely safe, but also destructive to declarer's plan. A forcing defence is so easy, yet, for some reason, less experienced players are put off leading a suit that the declarer will trump. Don't be.

Entry-Killing Plays

We move from a reminder that passive defence is often the most profitable, especially against suit contracts, to a super-aggressive form of defence, but one that makes sense, since, in each case, the declarer is trying to set up a long suit.

Playing the long suit early

It is very, very rare that it is right for the defenders to lead dummy's long suit. But, when that long suit is contained in a dummy with no outside entries, and the defence know that they, currently, have control of the hand, this could be the time to cut communications between declarer and the table.

```
Dealer South        ♠ 872
Love All            ♥ 10
                    ♦ AKQJ52
                    ♣ 1076

    ♠ Q1063              N            ♠ 94
    ♥ K74           W         E       ♥ 653
    ♦ 83                 S            ♦ 1097
    ♣ AK52                            ♣ Q9843

                    ♠ AKJ5
                    ♥ AQJ982
                    ♦ 64
                    ♣ J
```

N	E	S	W
–	–	1H	NB
2D	NB	2S	NB
3D	NB	**4H**	

West leads A♣, and is encouraged by East's 9♣. From the bidding, West knows that South is at least 6-4 in hearts and spades and that, as West holds ♠ Q1063, declarer holds spade losers; only the diamond suit offers South salvation. South has at least one club, and so will not hold more than two diamonds. If West switches to a diamond now, and then, when she regains the lead with K♥ later, leads another diamond, declarer will be stuck in dummy – not having drawn West's last trump – and will have no diamonds left in hand. Crucially, as West holds a certain natural trump trick, she knows that she is in control of the hand.

This defence – and no other – dooms the contract.

Please do not look at this example and think that leading dummy's long suit is an acceptable, regular occurrence. It is usually the wrong defence, even if you lead a singleton. Leading dummy's long suit almost always helps the declarer.

Attacking entries

Once you are familiar with – and used to watching – your opponents routinely setting up dummy's long suit by ruffing, you should be constantly imagining what the declarer might be planning to do. As a defender, your job is to thwart that plan.

Dealer South
Love All

	♠ 752	
	♥ Q98	
	♦ A9743	
	♣ KJ	

♠ KJ86		♠ Q103
♥ 5	N W E S	♥ 63
♦ 1082		♦ KQ65
♣ 109863		♣ AQ52

	♠ A94	
	♥ AKJ10742	
	♦ J	
	♣ 74	

N	E	S	W
–	–	1H	NB
2D	NB	3H	NB
4H			

West leads 10♣. East should not grab her winners, but instead study the table. Dummy offers the declarer two chances to make extra tricks. Declarer might be able to ruff a club – maybe two clubs – in dummy; she might be able to set up dummy's diamond suit, using dummy's three high trumps as entries, to make the fifth diamond a winner.

Let's just play that second scenario out. East takes her clubs and switches to a spade: this looks sensible, leading around to weakness. But, South wins A♠, plays J♦ to A♦, and ruffs a diamond high in hand. She leads 2♥ to 8♥ on the table, and ruffs a second diamond high in hand. She plays 4♥ to 9♥ in dummy and plays a fourth diamond, ruffing out East's last honour. Finally, South plays 7♥ to dummy's Q♥ and cashes her fifth diamond, throwing away a spade loser. Contract made.

East's job is to imagine this scenario and put a stop to it. The way to do that is to attack the entries to dummy's long suit before declarer wants to use them. East should win trick one and switch promptly to a trump. This takes a vital entry out of dummy and prevents South from being able to set up the long diamonds. If South's hand had been different, this switch also cuts down South's ability to ruff club losers in dummy.

Take the time to imagine the declarer's likely plan, and then seek to thwart it.

The Merrimac Coup

The *Merrimac* was a merchant ship deliberately sunk in 1898 at the mouth of a Cuban harbour in an attempt to seal it up and strand the Spanish fleet. Such a sacrifice lies at the heart of this entry-killing style of play.

Dealer South
Love All

	♠ 65	
	♥ J63	
	♦ KJ10943	
	♣ A7	

	N		♠ A73
W		E	♥ Q984
	S		♦ Q5
			♣ K864

N	E	S	W
–	–	1H	NB
2D	NB	2NT	NB
3NT			

West leads J♠. What should East be thinking about?

Dummy's long diamond suit will be vital to the success of declarer. If South holds A♦, East must hope that she finesses into her hand, and that the attack on spades proves lucrative.

East therefore overtakes J♠ with A♠ and returns 7♠, South winning with Q♠. South now leads 7♦, West plays 2♦, and J♦ is played from dummy.

East wins with Q♦ and realises that, if South had held A♦, she would almost certainly have played it first. So, if West holds A♦, there is a good chance that declarer can be cut off from the dummy.

East should also note that West played 2♦ – indicating an odd number of cards (almost certainly three) in diamonds. If West had held ♦A2, she might well have risen with the ace immediately.

So, East must attack dummy's one side entry to the long diamond suit. Leading a low club might allow South to win in hand with Q♣, but leading K♣, while giving up a trick in clubs, might end up saving four tricks in diamonds. When East leads K♣, if declarer ducks, East continues clubs. If declarer wins with A♣ immediately, her entry is blown before she can use it.

Here's the full deal:

Dealer South
Love All

```
                      ♠ 65
                      ♥ J63
                      ♦ KJ10943
                      ♣ A7
    ♠ J1098          ┌──────────┐        ♠ A73
    ♥ 102            │    N     │        ♥ Q984
    ♦ A62            │ W     E  │        ♦ Q5
    ♣ 10532          │    S     │        ♣ K864
                     └──────────┘
                      ♠ KQ42
                      ♥ AK75
                      ♦ 87
                      ♣ QJ9
```

East's switch to K♣ is the only defence to beat the contract and prevent South from establishing the diamond suit – and then enjoying her tricks.

There is a famous hand that is a more complex version of the Merrimac Coup, and it featured Oswald Jacoby – truly one of the greats of American bridge.

Dealer North	♠ 4
Love All	♥ 765
	♦ AJ3
	♣ KQJ1098

♠ J2
♥ 9842
♦ Q652
♣ A63

```
    N
W       E
    S
```

N	E	S	W
1C	1S	Dbl*	NB
2C	NB	**3NT**	

South's first bid is a Negative Double, indicating a four-card heart suit.

West leads J♠ and this is ducked by everyone else. What should West do now?

West realises that the club suit in dummy is crucial and wonders whether dummy's A♦ can be removed before declarer can use it to reach the established club winners. For this plan to succeed, East must hold K♦, or declarer can reach dummy twice, successfully finessing West for Q♦. To lead a low diamond here would simply allow South to run the lead around to her hand. East would win with K♦, but then could not lead a diamond back into dummy's ♦AJ without still leaving a winner.

West saw the light: he led Q♦! If declarer ducks in dummy, West continues leading diamonds until A♦ is knocked out; if declarer rises with A♦, when West takes his A♣ having exhausted South of her supply of clubs, South is cut off from the dummy hand and the contract is defeated.

Dealer North
Love All

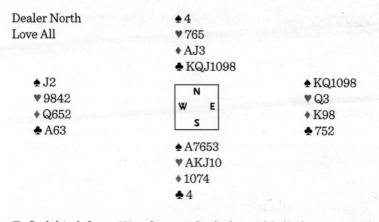

```
                        ♠ 4
                        ♥ 765
                        ♦ AJ3
                        ♣ KQJ1098
    ♠ J2                                      ♠ KQ1098
    ♥ 9842              N                      ♥ Q3
    ♦ Q652          W       E                  ♦ K98
    ♣ A63                S                     ♣ 752
                        ♠ A7653
                        ♥ AKJ10
                        ♦ 1074
                        ♣ 4
```

To find this defence, West foresaw the declarer's likely plan, imagined what card his partner would need to hold to mount a successful defence and, appreciating that East holding K♦ was perfectly possible, set about his plan to devastating effect.

Advanced Unblocking Situations

An early, and favourite, student of mine improved his game well over the years but could never bring himself to throw away high cards. It was, he claimed, a principle that ran contrary to how he led his life: you are dealt some good cards; you hang on to them.

This section should convince you otherwise.

To provide an entry for partner

If you have an entry, but no winner(s) to cash after gaining the lead, and your partner is in the opposite situation, set about trying to promote your partner's higher cards into winners by jettisoning yours.

This hand is a favourite of mine to test declarers on what is sometimes called a 'Stranding Play' but, all too often, the declarer prevails without having made the crucial play, just because the defenders are unfocused on what is happening and what they might do about it.

```
Dealer South          ♠ 85
Game All              ♥ A732
                      ♦ 8652
                      ♣ AKQ
    ♠ KQ1093                              ♠ J64
    ♥ 94              ┌─────────┐         ♥ QJ108
    ♦ J109           │    N     │         ♦ Q7
    ♣ 643           │  W   E   │          ♣ 10752
                     │    S     │
                     └─────────┘
                      ♠ A72
                      ♥ K65
                      ♦ AK43
                      ♣ J98
```

N	E	S	W
–	–	1D	NB
1H	NB	1NT	NB
3D*	NB	3S*	NB
3NT			

After South's 1NT rebid, North's jump to 3D was game-forcing, expressing concern about at least one of the unbid suits for no-trumps. South's 3S said, I have the spades covered, and so North could then bid 3NT.

Requiring an extra trick in diamonds, the correct line of play is for South to duck the spade leads until the third round, cross to dummy with Q♣ and lead a diamond. When East plays low, South must win, cross back to dummy with K♣ and lead another low diamond. This time, East must play Q♦, so declarer ducks, leaving East – with no spades left – stranded on lead.

It's a favourite hand of mine, but it keeps being spoilt when South cashes A♦ and then leads a low diamond from hand. Luckily for her, East must win, and declarer prevails. It's a terrible way to play the hand but, worse yet, it shows that East is paying no attention whatsoever.

The moment that East realises that West has spade winners to cash, she should be on a mission to throw every high card from her hand she can find. In this way, lower cards in West's hand might become winners and provide the crucial entry. To that end, as soon as a top diamond is laid down by South, East should drop her Q♦ immediately. That way, West's J♦ will inevitably win a diamond trick, and declarer can never prevail. From a teacher's point of view, South is punished for not finding the correct line of play. Try to make your teacher happy.

Playing high second-in-hand to freeze dummy's long suit

Lazily following the mantra of 'Second Plays Low' is fine for kitchen bridge players but, when you are trying to think about bridge, you will realise that, when there is a long suit in dummy, a high card in the second seat must often be sent in as a sacrifice to a higher good.

Dealer South   ♠ A95
Game All   ♥ 74
                                ♦ AJ10862
                                ♣ 83

        ♠ Q10873   ♠ K2
        ♥ J865   ┌─────────┐   ♥ 10932
        ♦ K4   │   N   │   ♦ Q97
        ♣ 74   │ W   E │   ♣ KQ109
                           │   S   │
                           └─────────┘
                                ♠ J64
                                ♥ AKQ
                                ♦ 53
                                ♣ AJ652

N	E	S	W
–	–	1C	NB
1D	NB	1NT	NB
3NT			

West leads 7♠, dummy plays low, East K♠ and declarer low. East
returns 2♠ and declarer ducks in dummy a second time before West
leads a third spade to clear the suit.

At many tables, the declarer will come to hand with A♥ and lead
3♦. West will follow small, dummy will insert J♦ and East will win Q♦.
Whatever East returns, South wins, leads a second diamond, beating
West's K♦ and running all the diamonds.

All West has to do is to realise that, if South has Q♦, her K♦ is
wastepaper (South would probably have led Q♦ anyway), and that if
East holds Q♦, by West playing K♦ immediately over 3♦, South is
forced to play her ace in dummy (if she ducks, West is on lead to cash
spade winners) and East can win her Q♦ on the next round, cutting
declarer off from the table.

Even if the diamonds were laid out like this . . .

                          ♦ AJ10862
                       ┌─────────┐
        ♦ K94   │   N   │   ♦ Q7
                       │ W   E │
                       │   S   │
                       └─────────┘
                          ♦ 53

... it would still, technically, be right – when South led a low diamond – for West to rise with K♦: the same effect is achieved.

In this instance, there is the possibility that East holds the singleton Q♦ but, if so, the contract will make anyway, so if you are trying to break the contract, it is definitely the right play.

This is the crux of this book: *think* about your play – preferably before the crucial trick arrives, but even then, think about what you are doing. Don't just play the card nearest to your thumb.

To avoid being endplayed

Sometimes it is very difficult to anticipate a complex play like an endplay when you are sitting in a defender's seat. However, at other times, you should be able to anticipate the declarer's plan and, if you remain alert, you can outwit her.

```
Dealer South              ♠ J32
Game All                  ♥ AQ963
                          ♦ 85
                          ♣ AK8
        ♠ 9875                              ♠ 1064
        ♥ 2            ┌─────────┐          ♥ 105
        ♦ KJ43        │    N     │          ♦ 109762
        ♣ QJ103       │ W     E  │          ♣ 952
                      │    S     │
                      └─────────┘
                          ♠ AKQ
                          ♥ KJ874
                          ♦ AQ
                          ♣ 764
```

N	E	S	W
–	–	1H	NB
2NT*	NB	3C*	NB
3H*	NB	3S*	NB
4C*	NB	4NT	NB
5S	NB	**6H**	

North's 2NT is a Jacoby-style Raise. South's 3C indicates a hand with five losers or fewer (a slightly optimistic reading of her hand); the next three bids are cue-bids indicating aces. Roman Key-Card Blackwood completed the questioning. Unfortunately for South, the hand is a complete 'duplication' – identical shape in both declarer and dummy's hands, leaving her with a club to lose and a diamond finesse to take. Declarer immediately spied a plan: on the lead of Q♣, she would win, draw trumps, eliminate spades, cash her other top club and throw West back on lead a low club. West would then have to lead a diamond around to South's ♦AQ. Most of the time, this plan will work ...

But, if West is alert, she will be aware that this is a possible plan by declarer and, on the second round of trumps, she will discard J♣ and, on the second round of clubs, she might throw 10♣. Now, when declarer tries to exit, it is East who wins with 9♣, and she can lead a diamond through the South hand to defeat the slam.

But what, you may ask, would happen if West threw away her top clubs and South held 9♣? South makes the slam – but, crucially, she would have made it anyway via the endplay, so you have lost nothing. And, anyway, as you get better at bridge, you have to be prepared to be humiliated and humbled when an expert play fails spectacularly.

The easiest time to drift off at the green baize is when you are defending with a terrible hand. Especially if you are playing Duplicate Pairs, but frankly at any time, if you can make one key play with your awful cards, you will be doing much better than anybody else.

Dealer West
Game All

	♠ 85	
	♥ AKJ7	
	♦ 7632	
	♣ AKQ	
♠ AKJ632	N	♠ 1097
♥ 54	W E	♥ 83
♦ KJ9	S	♦ 1054
♣ 104		♣ J9652
	♠ Q4	
	♥ Q10962	
	♦ AQ8	
	♣ 873	

N	E	S	W
–	–	–	1S
Dbl	NB	3H	NB
4H			

West leads ♠AK before switching to a club. Declarer has a diamond finesse which, from the bidding, is almost certainly wrong, and the third round of diamonds, which is losing. She plans an endplay similar to the previous hand. She draws trumps, cashes her other two top clubs and then leads 2♦ from dummy. East lazily follows low, and declarer puts in 8♦ from hand. West wins with 9♦ and is endplayed: if she plays another spade, this gives South a chance to ruff in dummy and discard a diamond from hand; if West leads a diamond, it plays straight back into declarer's ♦AQ.

Is the endplay breakable? Yes. When declarer leads 2♦ from dummy, East must rise with 10♦. South can put on Q♦ and West will win with K♦, but now West has ♦J9 and declarer ♦A8, so West can play a diamond, force out South's A♦, and make a diamond trick at the end.

To break up an endplay, when the declarer is attempting an exit, the second hand to play should play high to give the declarer as much trouble as possible.

3

BIDDING CONCEPTS

Far more important than playing conventions is to play them well, without partnership misunderstanding, leaving out elements that are worthless and including essentials that genuinely assist your side to judge the auction better.

At the end of this final part of the book is a convention card which covers an Acol-based system and which has proved powerful in competitions ranging from modest club duplicates to national championship standard. Whatever you decide to play, ensure that you and your partner are fluent in the use of all gadgets – bridge is a tough enough game without misunderstandings contributing terrible results to your overall score.

I first covered most of the conventions mentioned here in *Control the Bidding*, so, if you are new to any of these, you may want to look through that book before returning to this part.

Ultimately, whatever system you play, I hope that you will find ideas here that will contribute to both your enjoyment of, and success at, this most demanding of mind-sports.

3

BIDDING CONCEPTS

Weak and Strong Two Openers

To pre-empt freely with a weak hand is now part of everyday super-aggressive bidding. However, some systems suit Weak Two Openers better than others, and, for an Acol-based system, Weak Twos in the major suits fit beautifully, whereas Weak Twos in the minor suits interfere with a strong existing element of the system: the game-forcing opening bid.

Weak Twos in the minor suits often prove ineffective at preventing the opponents reaching the correct contract and, more importantly, once the opponents have got there, the information from the auction can lead declarer to make plays which, without the Weak Two Opener, they might never have made, resulting in contracts succeeding when, without the distributional information, they would fail, and overtricks made because of the knowledge of the opponents' hand patterns.

For these reasons, my preference is for 2H and 2S to be played as Weak openers, and 2C and 2D as Strong openers.

Weak 2H and 2S openers

In some systems, these may be played quite strong but, in Acol-based systems, it makes sense to play them properly weak. Five to nine points is a reasonable range, and this might include excellent four-counts and terrible ten-counts.

(a)	(b)	(c)
♠ KJ10984	♠ Q6	♠ A5
♥ 53	♥ KJ7432	♥ KQJ964
♦ 8532	♦ Q43	♦ 432
♣ 4	♣ Q7	♣ 75

(a) If this isn't worth a Weak 2S opening bid, I don't know what is! Great suit quality, lovely hand shape – definitely worth trying to disturb your opponents.

(b) An appalling 10-count, but probably worth an opening bid of 2H since, if your opponents buy the contract, they are likely to play your partner for the missing queens, hence you are combining a barrage with some deception.

(c) Too strong for a Weak 2H, this seven-loser 10-count offers six tricks opposite a reasonable hand.

Third-in-hand Weak Two (and Weak Three) openers

I have long found that opening the bidding at the one-level on a sub-minimum hand in third position leads to trouble: your partner is unable to judge competition, including – crucially at Pairs – when to double the opponents. However, opposite a passed hand, a pre-emptive bid is quite safe, since partner can do nothing but support your suit. For this reason, I recommend that a partnership agreement that pre-empts third-in-hand can be weaker or stronger than usual and – when non-vulnerable – one card shorter than usual. This maximises the pressure on your opponents while minimising the likelihood of your side suffering an embarrassingly large penalty.

This trump-length understanding must be clear, however, to prevent your partner from raising your pre-empt too high and hence providing your opponents with an easy decision to double you for penalties.

So, assuming that your side is non-vulnerable, after two passes, you might take the following action:

(d) ♠ KQJ109
♥ 75
♦ 42
♣ 7432

(e) ♠ A6
♥ 32
♦ AQJ10942
♣ 74

(f) ♠ QJ9843
♥ 4
♦ 432
♣ 752

(d) 2S. Your suit quality is perfect, and you have no defence to any reasonable contract your opponents may bid. This could keep them out of 3NT which, since you have no re-entry to your suit, they are likely to make.

(e) 3D. Too strong for a Weak Three usually, third-in-hand, to open 1D simply gives your opponents a chance to find their major-suit fit with ease. Now, the pressure is on them and, if your left-hand opponent (LHO) doesn't fancy overcalling 3H or 3S on a five-card suit, you might silence them altogether.

(f) 2S. Your opponents have a game contract available – for certain. You must, at least, attempt to bamboozle them. Whenever you open very light, simply ensure that you have your quality (however little of it you possess) in your long suit.

So, third-in-hand, non-vulnerable:

Weak Two Openers range from 3–11pts, and may be made on a five-card suit.
Weak Three Openers range from 3–12pts, and may be made on a six-card suit.

If you feel this is quite frisky, I have experienced the top players pre-empting at the three-level on five-card suits. This is the way of the modern game: aggression at all times, and so consistently that opponents are worn down by all the close decisions at high levels they are forced to make.

2NT opener

There is a trend to be able to show both a 19/20 and a 21/22pt balanced hand from the off. At Duplicate Pairs the showing of this lower range offers no advantage and often gets the partnership a big bottom.

For me, 19pt balanced hands (and poor 20pt hands) should be opened at the one-level and, if partner can dredge up a response, the rebid can show this strength.

So, a 2NT opener shows a good 20–22pts with a balanced-ish distribution.

At Teams of Four, missing a rare game could be very serious, so maybe you can indulge your 19pt urges with a strong opener then …?

Advanced responses to 2C opener

The Acol game-forcing 2C opener is a wonderful thing even in its basic form, but, when played with these simple additional responses, it becomes even more powerful, which is another reason why I prefer to keep 2C and 2D as strong bids, rather than playing them as weak.

In response to a 2C opening bid, which may be a balanced hand with 23pts or more, or a distributional hand with, generally, ten playing tricks (sometimes only nine playing tricks – see below), these should be your responses:

2D	Your hand contains an ace, or a king, or two queens with at least one connecting jack. There is no upper limit to your overall point count.
2H	Your hand does not contain an ace, or a king, or two queens with at least one connecting jack. (Some people play this bid to show 0–5pts, but that is ridiculous: a 2C opener wants to know if you have an ace or a king in your hand in order to explore safely whether there might be a slam available. 0–5 tells partner nothing!)
2S, 3C, 3D	This is your five-card suit or longer, which is headed by two of the top three honours. With a six- or seven-card suit, this could be headed by merely AJ or KJ.
2NT	You have a five-card heart suit, or longer, headed by two of the top three honours.

Over partner's instant double-negative 2H response, the 2C opener can immediately decide whether or not there is any chance of slam, without going beyond the game level.

Rebids of suits remain game-forcing; rebids of NT are standard: 2NT = 23/24pts; 3NT indicates 25pts plus.

Over partner's 2D response, game is now certain, so a 2NT rebid becomes unconditionally forcing to game and shows 23pts plus. This allows the responder to use Stayman and Transfers, and/or any other desired gadgets, at the three-level, hence improving the opportunities to find the best fit.

Slam can now be approached with the knowledge that responder holds some useful values.

This 2D response also frees up the 3NT rebid, which can now be used to show a nine playing trick hand based on a long minor suit.

West	East	West	East
♠ A6	♠ 983	2C	2D
♥ A9	♥ 7542	3NT	**6NT**
♦ AKQJ75	♦ 62		
♣ A43	♣ KQJ6		

After East's 2D response, West rebids 3NT directly to indicate a nine-trick hand based on a long minor suit, with a stopper in each suit. East must reckon that his clubs will provide three further tricks, and can therefore bid 6NT immediately. If West had held, say, K♠ also, he could then move to 7NT.

Keeping the fully positive responses of 2S, 2NT (showing hearts), 3C and 3D as five-card suits headed by two of the top three honours (unless you have extra length, when the quality may be compromised slightly) is a little restrictive, but it can lead to bidding slams easily. At club level, partnership confidence is all and there is no doubt that this restriction enhances that.

West	East	West	East
♠ AJ6	♠ KQ874	2C	2S
♥ A3	♥ J54	**7NT**	
♦ AJ	♦ 732		
♣ AKQJ73	♣ 65		

This has to be the easiest grand slam ever. Over the years, my partner and I have encountered many hands like this. These methods make judging the level easy.

The agreement only to show a positive with a five-card suit headed by two of the top three honours does not preclude the showing of a suit without such good quality.

West	East	West	East
♠ A62	♠ KJ874	2C	2D
♥ A3	♥ 982	2NT	3H*
♦ AKQJ	♦ 653	3S	3NT
♣ AQ73	♣ 94	**4S**	

After West's 2NT (23pts plus) rebid, East uses a Transfer to show his five-card spade suit. Knowing that East cannot hold both K♠ and Q♠ (since he would have given a positive 2S response initially), West can opt for the safer 4S contract, knowing that he may have a spade loser.

Finally, since following a 2D response the 2NT rebid by the opener is unlimited, both members of the partnership should be familiar with the principle of a Quantitative Raise.

West	East	West	East
♠ KQ3	♠ A87	2C	2D
♥ AJ	♥ 954	2NT	4NT
♦ AK104	♦ Q832	**6NT**	
♣ AKJ7	♣ Q95		

When West rebids 2NT, he shows 23pts plus. East, with 8pts, should count that, opposite a flat 23/24-count, his hand is unlikely to provide enough to make a small slam but, opposite 25pts or more, the partnership total hits 33pts plus, making 6NT a good bet. A Quantitative Raise to 4NT asks opener to pass with a minimum (23/24) but continue to 6NT with 25pts or more.

If West actually holds 28pts or more, he can take a deep breath and bid 7NT.

Strong 2D opener

Playing a 2D opener as I suggest is not a brilliant addition to your system, but it is probably the best use of the bid, and can prove powerful. Playing 2D as weak, however, affects the 2C opener also and, as discussed previously, it really isn't a good tool to upset your opponents. Incidentally, when you pick up one of the hands shown at the end of this section, you will love playing 2D like this. They don't come up that often, but they do appear, and when they do, this is a lovely gadget to have at your disposal.

An opening bid of 2D shows a strong hand:

- either containing a high-quality six-card suit or longer, worth eight or nine playing tricks;
- or a 4-4-4-1 hand containing 19pts or more.

The opener's rebid indicates which type of hand it is:

- the rebid of a suit shows the single-suited hand type;
- and the rebid of 2NT shows the 4-4-4-1 hand type.

Since the standard responder's 2H relay (and occasional break of the relay), plus the opener's single-suited hand type, is covered in *Control the Bidding*, I want to focus on the innovation of being able to show strong 4-4-4-1 hands.

Following the likely 2H relay, opener's rebid of 2NT indicates a 4-4-4-1 hand with 19pts of more. Partner then bids her longest suit – usually prioritising a four-card major over a longer minor, especially at Duplicate Pairs. If this suit is the opener's singleton, she rebids 3NT, and the bidding stops or progresses from there.

If the responder's suit hits one of the opener's four-card suits, the opener can choose between these two bids:

- With a minimum hand – say 19–20pts – she raises the suit one level.
- With a maximum hand – say 21pts plus – she bids her singleton as a Splinter.

This allows the responder to make an informed decision to settle for game or proceed to a slam. It does mean that a responder with a super-weak hand (0–3pts) is likely to end at too high a level, but at least the denomination will be correct, and if the responder's meagre points are opposite the opener's length, a slim game may yet be made. Let's see some examples:

West	East	West	East
♠ KQJ6	♠ A74	2D*	2H*
♥ AQJ7	♥ K983	2NT*	3H
♦ 4	♦ 9873	4D*	**6H**
♣ AKJ2	♣ Q5		

Following East's 2H relay, West indicates her 4-4-4-1 hand with her 2NT rebid. Prioritising her four-card major, East bids 3H. With a fit and a non-minimum hand, West Splinters with a bid of 4D, allowing

East to realise that all her points are working. Now, she could use cue-bids or Blackwood, or simply punt the perfect slam. Try bidding that contract without this method.

West	East	West	East
♠ 6	♠ 9874	2D*	2H*
♥ AKQ3	♥ 54	2NT*	3S
♦ A854	♦ 73	**3NT?**	**5C?**
♣ AQ72	♣ K8643		

East has an awful hand but, having relayed with 2H, then prioritises her four-card major initially, West rebids 3NT to indicate that her singleton is in spades. Now East could settle for a safe 5C or stand 3NT and hope that spades break or, since she has bid them, are not led. 6C might make without a trump lead, but who will be bidding that?

West	East	West	East
♠ KJ106	♠ Q874	2D*	2H*
♥ 3	♥ J542	2NT*	3H
♦ AKQJ	♦ 8732	3NT	**4S**
♣ KQJ7	♣ 6		

Another dismal hand for East who first relays, then shows her heart suit and finally, when West indicates that this is her singleton, converts to the known 4-4 spade fit. Note that East ignores her minor suit and, had she had a stronger hand, would have had to bid 5S or 6S, since West will always pass the conversion of one game contract to another.

Transfers for Minor-Suit Slams

3S Transfer opposite 2NT opener, and over 2C-2D-2NT

While we are dealing with strong openings and responses, let's add one further Transfer to our repertoire.

Many people play 1NT–2S as a Transfer indicating a long minor suit with thoughts of a slim NT contract but, however you play that bid, there is a 3S Transfer available opposite a 2NT opener or a 2C–2D–2NT sequence, which helps you to look for slim minor-suit slams.

Opposite a 2NT opener, or a rebid of 2NT after a 2C opener, 3S indicates a hand with at least 5-4 in the minor suits and values for a slim slam or more (let's say at least 30pts between you, opposite the mid-range for partner's bid).

If the opener has most of her values in the major suits, she will return to 3NT, after which you will pass, make a Quantitative Raise or, if more distributional than 5-4, bid on in the minors.

If the opener has aces and kings in the major suits and length support in one or both minors, she will show preference and allow you to investigate for a slam via cue-bids or Blackwood.

Let's take a look at a few examples of this Transfer in action:

West	East	West	East
♠ AQJ8	♠ 4	2NT	3S*
♥ AQJ6	♥ 843	**3NT**	
♦ QJ	♦ K743		
♣ K92	♣ AQ843		

East uses the 3S Transfer to indicate at least 5-4 in the minor suits. West, who is strong in the majors and rich in queens and jacks (which are useful far more in no-trumps than suit contracts), rebids 3NT, which East passes.

West	East	West	East
♠ A832	♠ 4	2NT	3S*
♥ AK6	♥ 843	4D	**6D**
♦ AQJ8	♦ K7432		
♣ K5	♣ AQ84		

Opposite a similar East hand, this time West holds aces and kings in the majors and support for diamonds, so she shows a desire to play in a diamond slam. East could cue-bid or use Blackwood, but it will be tough to discern West's overall shape and trick-taking potential so, despite 13 tricks being likely to make, bidding 6D will still be a fine result.

West	East	West	East
♠ AKJ8	♠ 4	2C*	2D
♥ AKQ3	♥ J75	2NT	3S*
♦ A6	♦ K7432	3NT	4NT
♣ KJ2	♣ A1097	**6NT**	

West declines East's minor-suit slam suggestion but, when she rebids 3NT, East realises that West's range is 23pts <u>plus</u>, and she therefore makes a Quantitative Raise asking West to bid 6NT if she is non-minimum. In this context 23/24 is minimum and 25pts plus is maximum, so West bids 6NT. On a spade or club lead, the slam is home; on a red-suit lead, West should probably duck a round of diamonds and then test them for a 3-3 break. If that fails, having cashed hearts, decide against whom to finesse for Q♣.

The sequence 2C–2H–2NT–3S is unlikely to occur since the 2H response to 2C indicates an extra-bad hand. If used, it might show 5-5 or longer in the minor suits, seeking a safer 5C/5D contract as opposed to 3NT.

And, since we are investigating minor-suit slams, let's add this to our existing Transfers.

Indicating a minor two-suited hand after a 1NT opener

However you choose to play 1NT–2S (I like it to show 9/10pts with a decent-quality six-card minor – see *Control the Bidding*), if, over partner's 2NT relay – should this be part of your system – you then bid 3S, this shows a hand with 5-5 or greater in the two minor suits, with a desire to play at five-, six- or seven-level in a minor suit.

West	East	West	East
♠ A64	♠ 5	1NT	2S*
♥ K743	♥ AJ	2NT*	3S*
♦ Q10	♦ KJ987	4C	**6C**
♣ KJ32	♣ AQ864		

West agrees clubs as she holds length and good stuffing in the minor suits and quick trick values in the majors. There is no room for Blackwood, and a 4H cue-bid is unlikely to elicit any crucial information, so East punts the slam – and an excellent one it is too.

West	East	West	East
♠ QJ97	♠ 84	1NT	2S
♥ KJ5	♥ Q	2NT*	3S*
♦ A62	♦ KQJ32	**3NT**	
♣ J53	♣ AKQ74		

West indicates poor support for the minors and good enough major-suit holdings to play in no-trumps opposite singletons in those suits. East is not quite strong enough to make a Quantitative Raise, and passes.

If East is 6-5 in the minors, over a 3NT rebid by the opener she can bid her six-card minor and force opener to select a minor, but, especially at Duplicate Pairs, 3NT must be bypassed only when it seems a hopeless contract.

West	East	West	East
♠ KJ105	♠ 42	1NT	2S*
♥ QJ98	♥ –	2NT*	3S*
♦ A5	♦ KQ7432	3NT	4D
♣ Q32	♣ AKJ85	5C	**6C**

With her 6-5-2-0 distribution, East decides not to stand 3NT but to bid 4D to indicate 6-5 in diamonds and clubs. West selects clubs and East may be tempted to pass. However, at Duplicate, if 3NT was making with an overtrick, as it might well, 5C making or 5C+1 will not score well. On that basis, East should probably punt the small slam and hope to collect all the matchpoints on the deal. 6C isn't a terrible contract.

If North leads a spade, all is easy; if she does not, this may mark her with A♠; if your opponent leads a trump, you may well be able to draw trumps, rattle off six diamonds and learn a great deal about the position of the A♠ and Q♠.

At Duplicate Pairs, if you think that 3NT was probably making with overtricks, don't settle for 5C or 5D, since even if you make these contracts, they will score very poorly. Bid on to the six level. Bidding the small slam risks converting, say, a 10 per cent result into 0 per cent one, whereas should you make the slam, that 10 per cent is converted to 100 per cent – a risk offering you very good odds which you should often take.

Advance Cue-Bids

Where experts gain one of their advantages is through their ability to use bidding space to impart extra information, without bypassing the best contract. In the use of Advance Cue-Bids, a player can indicate a hand which is too strong merely to settle for game, but not strong enough to launch into a full-blooded slam investigation. This is a consultative bid – and such bids allow the partnership to use its' combined brain power to reach the best contract.

Let's take a look at a simple but important example:

West	East	West	East
♠ AQJ986	♠ K32	1S	2D
♥ KQ8	♥ A75	3S	4C*
♦ A	♦ J9874	4NT	5C*
♣ 743	♣ A8	5NT	**6S**

East is far too strong merely to bid 4S over West's forcing 3S jump-rebid. Her bid of 4C shows spade support (a doubleton containing ace or king or three-card support) plus the A♣ or a club void. It also indicates a hand where slam is possible.

West might continue cue-bidding or, as here, launch into RKCB. West asks for kings since, if East holds either K♣ or K♦, 7S is likely to be a decent contract.

As it is, 6S requires only a club ruff in dummy, or the establishment of one extra diamond trick, to succeed.

The next example can be played as either a Splinter (see *Control the Bidding*) or as an Advance Cue-Bid. However, you don't really need to define which this is. It shows either a singleton or a void, or the ace, plus agreement for the suit last bid.

West	East	West	East
♠ AK632	♠ 85	1S	2D
♥ AQ103	♥ KJ98	2H	4C*
♦ K5	♦ AJ743	4NT	5C*
♣ 43	♣ A8	5NT	**6H**

East's 4C bid is either a Splinter (singleton or void club) or A♣, but, crucially, it shows four-card heart support and an opening hand or better. West should be encouraged. Opposite his two club losers, a singleton or A♣ is great news, partner probably holds only one or two spades – with three-card support, he might use Fourth Suit Forcing (4SF) to investigate further – and West's K♦ looks a big card.

In fact, when East bids 5C, West might well decide to bid 7H. If East holds a singleton A♣, he is marked with six diamonds and there are then unlikely to be any losers that cannot be discarded on long diamonds or ruffed in dummy. Even with the hands as they are, 7H is a decent spot. However, reaching 6H seems pretty good – if East had simply leapt to 4H, that would surely have ended the auction.

Once you have limited your hand with, say, a no-trump rebid, you can still indicate suitability for progress:

West	East	West	East
♠ A986	♠ 32	1H	2C
♥ KJ86	♥ –	3NT	4D
♦ KJ	♦ AQ952	4S*	**6C**
♣ AQ5	♣ KJ8643		

When West makes a basic Acol rebid of 3NT to indicate 17–19/20pts, East continues with 4D, indicating 6-5 in clubs and diamonds (with 5-4 in those suits, East would pass 3NT or continue in no-trumps).

West's 4S bid is an Advance Cue-Bid, indicating A♠ and a hand particularly suitable for slam – made up predominantly of aces, kings, and values in partner's suits. This bid would usually agree the last bid suit by East but, here, with East showing 6-5 shape, it shows agreement for at least one of partner's suits.

East could investigate further but a small slam seems pretty solid, whereas judging a grand will be very tough. East bids 6C, expecting West to convert to 6D if she holds four-card support there.

Jacoby-Style Raises

There are many styles of forcing response to 1H and 1S openers, but some suit Acol-based systems better than others. Here, I suggest playing a non-game-forcing 2NT raise, with shape-showing descriptions.

Whatever style you decide to play, ensure that you have discussed not only the initial response, but also the relays, rebids and action after interventions. Very often I discover that people play conventions, but know only the first part of them. In those cases, it is usually detrimental to the partnership to be playing the convention at all.

Jacoby-style Raises

In response to a 1H or 1S opening bid – and without interference from the opponents – 2NT is played as a strong raise with four-card support, indicating about 10–15pts, up to the strength played for a strong jump-shift. As you are likely to be playing Splinters, the use of the 2NT raise suggests that most often your hand will not contain a singleton or void. However, when your singleton is a king or queen, you might decide not to Splinter but opt for a Jacoby-style Raise instead.

The Losing Trick Count (which is at its best for 4-4 and 5-4 trump fits) should be applied here, ensuring that you include the key adjustments (see page 130) for the most accurate representation of your hand.

We can now examine how this innovation should affect your raising values (in response to 1H or 1S opening bids).

1H–**2H**	3–6pts with four-card support (good ten-loser hand)
	5–9pts with three-card support (nine-loser hand)
1H–**3H**	7–10pts with four-card support (good nine-loser / bad eight-loser hand)
1H–**2NT**	Jacoby-style Raise
	10–15pts (eight losers or fewer), unlikely to contain singleton / void
1H–**3NT**	Pudding Raise
	12–15pts, four-card support, likely 3-3-3 in outside suits with one stopper or better in each suit
1H–**Splinter**	10–15pts, four-card support, singleton or void (usually six to seven losers)
1H–**4H**	0–9pts, very distributional
1H–**Jump-Shift**	16pts-ish, slam interest distributional hand (usually five losers or fewer)

Notice that both the 1H–2H raise and the 1H–3H raise are now more pre-emptive in style. Opener must be a little stronger than in standard Acol to push on towards game. The Losing Trick Count, combined with point count, should be applied here.

Opener's rebid following a Jacoby-style 2NT response

With the suit agreed, further description of your hands can now begin immediately. The opener has the first opportunity to describe her hand further. In these examples, let's have spades as the agreed suit.

After the auction 1S – 2NT, these are opener's available rebids:

3C   **Slam Interest**, forcing to game, showing five losers or fewer, with a minimum of five cards in the suit opened. Unless partner is minimum for her raise, she should now start to cue-bid immediately.

Because the sequence is forcing to game, if the responder is completely minimum for her Jacoby Raise, she jumps to game immediately. If she is not minimum, but has no ace or void to cue-bid (you are unable to cue-bid the trump ace), she can rebid 3S, which is the stronger option.

3D	**Six-loser hand or better, showing a singleton or void.** Having indicated a hand of intermediate strength, if the Jacoby Raiser now wishes to explore for slam, she can ask in which suit you hold your singleton by bidding 3H (whether or not this is the agreed suit). The opener now bids the suit in which she holds her shortage.
3S	**Minimum opening hand**, indicating a seven-loser hand with no redeeming features. The Jacoby bidder now passes with a minimum hand, or continues with a better hand.
4S	**Six-loser hand, with minimum values**, often based on having a six-card trump suit and good shape.
3NT	**Balanced hand,** 15–poor 20pts. Usually 4-3-3-3 or 4-4-3-2. This bid is designed to suggest a lack of ruffing values which, opposite a balanced Jacoby Raise, may well play better in a NT contract. If the Jacoby Raiser responder now bids 4NT, this is a Quantitative Raise, asking opener to pass with 15–17pts, and bid 6NT with 18–poor 20pts. If the Jacoby Raiser wishes to agree spades and use Blackwood, she should make a cue-bid over the 3NT bid, which sets the suit as spades, and then use 4NT subsequently.

Jump-Rebid in New Suit

This is a natural rebid, with six losers or fewer, showing 5-5 or longer in the two suits. The second suit should be headed by either ace or king, to ensure that Blackwood or cue-bidding can commence in the knowledge that first- or second-round control is present.

Since the opener will not open 1H with 5-5 in spades and hearts, a rebid of 3S following the 1H–2NT sequence would promise 6-5 in hearts and spades.

Similarly, following the sequence 1S–2NT, a rebid of 4C would show 6-5 in spades and clubs, since the opener will open 1C with 5-5 in spades and clubs.

Following the auction 1S–2NT, this is what the opener would rebid:

(a)	♠ AK8543	**(b)**	♠ AJ74	**(c)**	♠ AQ953
	♥ A3		♥ K82		♥ 4
	♠ AQ7		♦ AQ3		♦ KQ72
	♣ 43		♣ QJ7		♣ Q84
(d)	♠ AJ742	**(e)**	♠ AQ986	**(f)**	♠ KQJ632
	♥ Q53		♥ 2		♥ 94
	♠ Q82		♦ KQ743		♦ A832
	♣ K6		♣ Q7		♣ 5

(a) 3C. With a four- or good five-loser hand, there is slam potential here.

(b) 3NT. With a totally balanced hand, there is no guarantee that a spade contract will be superior to a NT contract.

(c) 3D. This indicates a singleton or void in your hand, with six losers or fewer. If the Jacoby Raiser wishes to discover in which suit you hold your shortage, she will bid 3H.

(d) 3S. A complete minimum.

(e) 4D. A non-minimum hand with 5-5 or longer in the two bid suits. The second suit must be headed by ace or king.

(f) 4S. Minimum values, six losers, often based on a six-card suit. Incidentally, this hand is far too strong to open a Weak 2S, even if your range includes 10pts – this is a six-trick hand.

Let's take a look at some possible auctions to see how the system works to help you reach the best contracts.

West	East	West	East
♠ 76	♠ AK3	1H	2NT*
♥ AKJ93	♥ 87542	4D	4NT
♦ AQ652	♦ K9	5C	**7H**
♣ 4	♣ A86		

This deal occurred in a club duplicate recently and few pairs managed to reach 7H. However, the opener's rebid, showing 5-5 in hearts and diamonds, meant that, when East used RKCB and discovered three key-cards in West's hand (West must have at least A♦ since her 4D rebid guaranteed either ace or king in her second suit), East could bid 7H with great confidence, since she knew that her A♣, ♠AK covered the three outside cards, and ♥AK and A♦ ensured that there would be no losers that could not be ruffed out.

West	East	West	East
♠ A86	♠ J53	1H	2NT*
♥ AQ103	♥ KJ95	3NT	4NT
♦ K94	♦ AJ108	**6NT**	
♣ KQ8	♣ A10		

East's 4NT is a Quantitative Raise, realising that opposite a strong flat hand (15–poor 20pts), ♣A10 may not be a useful ruffing value.

Notice that 6H and 6NT are virtually identical contracts – there is no club ruff, and you must find Q♦ to make twelve tricks. For Pairs scoring, better that those are in no-trumps than in hearts.

West	East	West	East
♠ AQJ652	♠ K873	1S	2NT*
♥ 52	♥ A98	3C*	3H*
♦ 3	♦ Q974	4C*	4S
♣ AQJ7	♣ K8	4NT	5H
		6S	

West's 3C rebid indicates five losers or fewer and asks East to begin cue-bidding if not minimum for her Jacoby-style Raise. East holds a bad six-loser hand, but it does contain slam-going aces and kings. The heart cue-bid reassures West that there are not two quick losers there, but the 5H response to RKCB confirms that there is a key-card missing. West can draw trumps, cash four rounds of clubs, pitching two hearts from East, and then ruff a heart in dummy for her twelfth trick.

Naturally, there will be plenty of occasions when, following a Jacoby Raise, there is no slam contract, but almost all of the time, game will result. Playing the 2NT as forcing to game, however, leaves a gap in our Acol auction, which is why this method works well.

Action after intervention

After an intervention by your opponents following the 1H or 1S opening bid, I recommend that you play that all your actions become natural (you can agree otherwise with a partner). With a strong raise in partner's suit, it is recommended that you cue-bid your opponent's suit at the lowest available level, or use a Splinter in their suit.

Your partner opens 1H, RHO overcalls 1S. What would you reply?

(a)	♠ KJ53	(b)	♠ 643	(c)	♠ 5
	♥ 53		♥ KJ74		♥ QJ96
	♠ K32		♦ KQ32		♦ A932
	♣ AJ72		♣ A7		♣ AJ75

(a) 2NT. Natural, indicating two stoppers in spades, a good 10–12pts.
(b) 2S. The simple cue-bid of your opponent's suit shows four-card support for hearts with a good 10pts, or eight losers, or better.
(c) 3S. The jump in your opponent's suit is a Splinter, agreeing hearts.

If your opponents bid a suit after partner has responded with 2NT, as opener you should compete as follows. You are sitting South.

N	E	S	W
–	–	1S	NB
2NT*	3C	?	

Pass	Indicates a minimum opener, with a five-card suit.
4S	Shows a minimum opener with a six-card suit (probably only six losers).
Double	Shows a singleton or void in the overcalled suit.
New Suit	Is natural, a four-card suit or longer, with six losers or fewer.
3NT	Shows 15pts or more, balanced, with ace or king in opponent's suit.

The requirement for ace or king in the opponent's suit to bid 3NT is there to ensure that your opponents – who, knowing that you have a fit and thus being able to compete freely – do not talk you out of a slam. This way, there is no concern about controls in their suit. This is slightly restrictive but 3NT is unlikely to be the best contract when you have a major-suit fit and your opponents have overcalled at the three-level.

If your opponents overcall at the four-level or higher:

Pass indicates a five-card suit, with minimum or near-minimum values.

Bidding on in your suit shows a six-card suit, with six losers or fewer.

Double indicates that your major is a four-card suit (and, inevitably, 15pts or more).

Any double by the Jacoby Raiser should be played for penalties.

With these arrangements in place, you now have a simple but powerful method of raising accurately when strong, and pre-emptively when weak. Exactly as it should be.

Losing Trick Count

Most readers will either be aware of, or already regularly refer to, the Losing Trick Count. However, there seem to be many players out there using it at the wrong time, misunderstanding its strengths and weaknesses, and failing to make even the key basic adjustments. So, here, we'll revise the technique and ensure that you can use it most effectively.

The origins of the LTC date back over a century, to a time when trick assessment was the only method of valuing your hand. These days, the LTC should be used in conjunction with point counts, knowledge of fit, and the opponents' bidding.

There are also some new theories and adaptations of the LTC, some of which seem genuine improvements on the standard ideas, but they are complex and not fully tested yet, so let's get the standard form of LTC to work as best as we can for us.

The LTC works very well for 4-4 fits, well for 5-4 fits, adequately for 5-3 fits and is pretty much useless the rest of the time. It should not be used to assess whether you should open the bidding, respond in a new suit or even overcall. Its prime use is to decide how high to support your partner, and how much further to bid having been supported.

Basic ideas

To assess the LTC value of your hand, assume that every suit should be headed by AKQ. Each one of these cards that is missing is worth one loser, up to the number of cards held in the suit. So, if you hold a singleton, you look only for the ace; you cannot have more than one loser; with a doubleton, look only for the ace, king; you cannot have more than two losers.

♠ KQ76	If you open 1H, and your partner responds 1S, now
♥ AQ984	having established a fit, you can apply the LTC.
♦ A3	You have one loser in spades, one loser in hearts,
♣ Q5	one loser in diamonds, and two losers in clubs.

Once you decide to support partner's suit, or have been supported, you assess how many losers you have, and do some simple arithmetic, based on these primary assumptions:

An opening hand is assumed to contain seven losers or fewer (you often open a Weak NT (12–14pts) with more than seven losers, but rarely one-of-a-suit).

A responding hand, which does not jump, is assumed to have nine losers or fewer.

When you are supporting your partner, add the number of losers in your hand to the assumed number in your partner's hand, and subtract that total from 18. This gives you the level to which the LTC suggests you can safely bid.

West	East	West	East
♠ 743	♠ J92	1H	3H
♥ AK93	♥ QJ87	**NB**	
♦ AK65	♦ 94		
♣ J2	♣ KQ63		

West opens 1H and East counts three losers in spades, two losers in hearts, two losers in diamonds and one loser in clubs. This totals eight losers. Adding eight losers to the opener's assumed seven losers = 15. This subtracted from 18, gives the answer 3.

West holds seven losers and so has no reason to bid on, and passes. 3H is the correct contract.

West	East	West	East
♠ KQ94	♠ J873	1D	1S
♥ 93	♥ A74	**4S**	
♦ AKQJ2	♦ 83		
♣ 43	♣ A982		

West opens 1D and East responds 1S, which West assumes to show a four-card spade suit or longer, 6pts or more, and nine losers or fewer. West adds up her losers: one in spades, two in hearts, none in diamonds and two in clubs, making a total of five losers. This added to the presumed nine losers in East's hand = 14. Taken away from 18, the answer is 4, making the raise to 4S the correct answer.

East does indeed have nine losers and, not playing the LTC, I wonder whether West would have bid only 3S and East might then have passed? If so, chalk one up to the Losing Trick Count.

These are the basic principles of the LTC: a trick estimation technique which sensibly downgrades the value of jacks – in fact, in this basic form, ignores them entirely – and values distribution. As an additional check to your point-count system, and your gut instinct about the value of a hand, it is a useful tool. It is excellent also for use during a Jacoby Raise sequence, as often the LTC will indicate whether there is the potential for a slam. It is not, however, particularly reliable at the five-, six- and seven-levels, and should be used only as a guide.

But, as mentioned earlier, there are some problems with this basic understanding, not least of which might be this:

A63   is two losers, as is   Q54

Clearly, the ace will always make a trick, and the queen only sometimes. To value both holdings as two losers seems unnecessarily inaccurate.

A72   is two losers, as is   AJ10

The ace holding can only make one trick; the ace-jack-ten holding is very likely to make two.

Because of these anomalies, let's take a look at some of the key adjustments you should make if you are to include this method of hand evaluation in your armoury.

Key adjustments to the LTC

1 If you hold a nine-card fit or longer, deduct one loser from the suit.

2 Qxx counts as two and a half losers (but only two losers if in the trump suit); Axx counts as one and a half losers.

3 AJ10 counts as one loser; KJ10 counts as one and a half losers.

The adoption of these adjustments will ensure that the LTC is as accurate as possible and will improve your bidding judgement. Without the adjustments, it is more likely to get you into trouble.

Using the LTC when responding to a take-out double

As even quite experienced players seem to have problems responding to a take-out double, consider applying the Losing Trick Count. You almost certainly have a 4-4, 5-4 or 5-3 fit, and the doubler almost always holds seven losers or fewer.

West	N	E	S	W
♠ K8643	1H	Dbl	NB	?
♥ 642				
♦ AK73				
♣ 5				

You have seven losers. If you are certain that your partner holds four-card spade support (she should do, but sometimes, quite reasonably, she doesn't) you can deduct a further loser. Even without that adjustment, your seven losers opposite the take-out doubler's seven losers = 14, subtracted from 18, means that 4S is the correct response.

Perhaps you would have made that bid anyway, or maybe you would have bid only 2S or 3S. Certainly, I would bid 4S, but not because of the LTC.

The hand is fitting very well. If partner is 4-1-4-4 with 12pts, I think that 4S will be an excellent spot. If she is less shapely, I expect a few more points. We probably have a double fit, which you should always assess as worth an extra trick (indeed, it usually is), and partner has a shortage in hearts and I have a club shortage, so there is cross-ruff potential too.

The point is this: don't let the Losing Trick Count – or any other gadget you play – become more important than thinking about bridge. This is the danger of *aide-mémoires*, flow charts, flippers and gadgets – they all distract from what you really need to be trying to do: thinking.

So use your gadgets and additional valuation techniques, like the LTC, in conjunction with your developing judgement, and not as a replacement.

Scramble

Natural and artificial uses of no-trump responses to a take-out double

There are many times when your partner makes a take-out double and you are faced with a decision as to which suit to respond. Most of the time, you can solve this problem using an Unassuming Cue-bid.

West	East	N	E	S	W
♠ J986	♠ KQ73	1D	Dbl	NB	*2D*
♥ K863	♥ A74				
♦ Q42	♦ 83				
♣ K3	♣ AJ82				

With a choice between majors, West can bid 2D, indicating two suits of the same rank, of similar quality, and sufficient points for at least the two-level. There is no upper limit for this bid, since the doubler is forced to choose suits – unless the original opener bids again – so West can adjust to the correct contract. Here, East will bid 2S and West will pass.

West	East	N	E	S	W
♠ QJ64	♠ AK5	1H	Dbl	2H	?
♥ 93	♥ 74				
♦ AQJ2	♦ K843				
♣ K43	♣ A982				

I know some experts like to play a UCB in this situation as well but, for most of the time, it simply leads to trouble. If you have a major and a minor, just get on and bid the major at the appropriate level. If your partner only has three-card support, you will have to play in a 4-3 fit but, since the hand with the shorter trumps is the one with the shortage in the opponent's suit, your trump suit should not come under undue pressure. Here, just bid 4S.

You will notice that 4S almost certainly makes, despite only seven trumps, whereas 5D has virtually no play.

By the way, while we're here: does a double of one major suit promise four cards in the other major? My answer is simple: yes, absolutely, unless the doubler only has three cards! Or, to put it another way, the doubler would *like* to have four cards in the other major.

West	East	N	E	S	W
♠ KQ84	♠ A953	1C	Dbl	3C	*4C*
♥ A764	♥ KQ9				
♦ Q2	♦ KJ843				
♣ 843	♣ 2				

East was right to double rather than to overcall 1D. If her five-card suit had been a major, then to overcall the major suit first would have been correct.

With all her values in her partner's long suits, West is strong enough to bid 4C here – still an Unassuming Cue-bid, indicating both majors. East should not bother to bid 4D, but simply choose between hearts and spades, alighting in 4S.

West	East	N	E	S	W
♠ AJ	♠ KQ73	1H	Dbl	NB	*2NT*
♥ QJ108	♥ 4				
♦ Q76	♦ AKJ10				
♣ J753	♣ Q942				

West does not want to bid 3C and, holding two solid stoppers in hearts, a no-trump contract certainly looks best. East, slightly stronger than minimum, is likely to raise to 3NT – which looks rock solid.

Responding no-trumps to a take-out double is never popular with the doubler since her shortage in the opponent's suit makes playing with a trump suit more desirable. However, sometimes it is the only, or clearly best, option.

Since, in a moment, we will see that to use a no-trump response to a take-out double is, in most other situations, artificial, let's clarify the situation in this last example.

When partner makes a take-out double on the first round of

bidding (even in the fourth-seat protective position – see next section), and the responding opponent does not bid, a response of no-trumps is natural, suggesting no long suit worth bidding and two stoppers in the opponent's suit. The point counts match those of NT responses to a one opening.

However, there are many occasions when a no-trump response cannot, logically, be natural and, in these situations, the bid becomes a 'Scramble'.

If in doubt, ask yourself whether a natural no-trump response could possibly make sense. Since the answer will almost always be no, you can then take the bid as the far more versatile Scramble.

West	East	N	E	S	W
♠ J4	♠ KQ96	1H	Dbl	3H	NB
♥ 932	♥ 8	NB	Dbl	NB	3NT
♦ Q982	♦ AK7				
♣ Q973	♣ KJ642				

Here, West would like to find out which minor suit East prefers, but does not have the values to bid 4H, escalating East's response to the five-level. Instead, here, a bid of 3NT cannot be natural since, if West really has two stoppers in hearts, she should pass out the double and take N/S for penalties. Additionally, since East has not promised a hugely strong hand for her second double – merely a well-shaped one – West would have to have close on an opening hand to bid 3NT naturally, but if she had that, she would have made some kind of bid on the previous round.

West's 3NT bid is therefore a Scramble, indicating the two minor suits. East shows a preference to clubs and 4C will usually make.

West	East	N	E	S	W
♠ Q65	♠ 3	–	1H	1S	NB
♥ 98	♥ AJ743	2S	Dbl	NB	2NT
♦ Q432	♦ KJ76				
♣ J973	♣ AQ2				

East reopens the auction with a take-out double and, again, West must decide what to do. Guessing which minor to bid could lead to an inferior contract so West makes a Scramble by bidding 2NT.

West cannot have 11 or 12pts, or she would have bid on the first round, so this is clearly artificial, asking East to choose between the two unbid suits. When East bids 3D, this has a decent chance of making.

West	East	N	E	S	W
♠ 653	♠ AK82	1D	Dbl	2D	NB
♥ 872	♥ QJ93	NB	Dbl	3D	NB
♦ 10862	♦ –	NB	Dbl	NB	*3NT*
♣ J53	♣ AQ987				

We all have hands like West's when partner will not shut up but, now, at least we do not have to guess. We could pass 3D doubled and hope that partner's weight of points and our four trumps will defeat our opponents, but since partner could have a hand where we could still make game, it is better that we bid. 3NT is obviously not to play, and we await partner's choice of suit in a relaxed state, since now partner will have to play the hand herself! Partner will bid 4C (since she should know that we do not hold a 4-card major suit) and this is not catastrophic, especially as 3D seems likely to be making despite the 4-0 trump break.

Bidding no-trumps in response to a fourth-seat protective double

In response to later-in-the-auction protective (or balancing) doubles, a no-trump bid is likely to be a Scramble. However, when responding to a first-round, fourth-seat protective double, a natural no-trump response could very well be desirable and, for that reason, it should be played as natural.

West	East	N	E	S	W
♠ J764	♠ AQ3	1H	NB	NB	Dbl
♥ 93	♥ Q1074	NB	*1NT*		
♦ KQ52	♦ J83				
♣ A63	♣ Q982				

East correctly passes over North's 1H opener and, when South also passes, West makes a protective take-out double. You and your partner should discuss the likely range of a double in this position, but I recommend playing it as the correct shape, with 9pts or more. On that basis, East must understand that her response must be adjusted. Applying the 'Theory of the Deferred Ace' (or King), deals with this just fine. Imagine that you have lent your partner an ace or king to make up her hand to a standard 12pt take-out double, and then make the normal response. Here, then, East takes away 3/4pts and responds 1NT, ensuring that the contract does not get too high. Obviously, if West has a stronger hand, she is entitled to raise this response accordingly.

I am tempted to say work out your point counts at the table, but since this book is designed to be helping you, let's just say this: opposite a take-out double in the fourth seat, a no-trump response is likely to have, roughly, these point counts:

1NT = 9–11pts
2NT = 12–14pts
3NT = 15pts or more.

Two observations: in these situations, the points division between the two partnerships will be, on average, 20–20, therefore if you hold fewer than 9pts, your partner is likely to hold an opening hand, so 1NT may still prove to be the best option, especially at Duplicate Pairs. For safety, with fewer than 9pts, you should bid a four-card suit instead of no-trumps, but you will have to use your at-the-table judgement to make this decision.

With 16pts or more, East might well have overcalled 1NT directly over North's initial opening bid, but there are hands of 15 and 16pts where pass is the correct option.

Splinters and Super-Splinters in Reverse Auctions

Here is a simple addition to your system which allows you to show, either with greater economy, or with more definition, your distributional hands with support for partner's suit.

One of the key understandings at bridge is that if a bid is natural and forcing, then a bid of that suit at the next higher level will not be natural. There are some exceptions where the jump bid is natural but promises greater length or particular strength but, generally, the policy is: why bid higher than you need to when your bid is already forcing? Take this auction:

West	East
1D	1S
2H	

The 2H rebid is a Reverse, showing 5-4 or longer in the two suits, with the equivalent of 16pts of more. It is forcing for one round. Even if the opener were 6-5, it would be best to describe her hand with this rebid, with a plan to bid hearts again at her next turn.

Therefore, this next auction is not natural:

West	East
1D	1S
3H	

And, if 3H is not natural, how should it be played?

What fits into our system most effectively is to play this jump-rebid as a Splinter, showing four-card spade support, a singleton heart, and sufficient values for at least a 3S contract and, in the real world, almost certainly a 4S contract.

So, when a simple rebid would be a forcing Reverse, a jump-rebid now becomes a Splinter agreeing partner's suit. Splinters must be used very carefully when agreeing a minor suit, as you don't want to bypass 3NT, especially at Duplicate Pairs, and some players keep Splinters simply for supporting major suits, but that is a decision for you and your partners.

If a single jump is forcing in these situations, what would a traditional Splinter double jump now indicate?

West	East
1D	1S
4H	

This can now be played as a Super-Splinter, indicating a void in hearts, with four-card spade support and a decent hand. Some people play that this can also show a singleton ace, but it is probably better to make a normal Splinter with such a holding and, if able, cue-bid your singleton ace later.

This hand came up just a couple of days before I wrote this section:

West	East	West	East
♠ J42	♠ A6	1C	1H
♥ AQ83	♥ K7542	*4D*	4NT
♦ –	♦ Q983	5S	5NT
♣ AK7542	♣ Q6	6C	**7H**

It's a fabulous hand for illustrating the Super-Splinter. When East responds 1H, although West has a relatively low point count, her hand is definitely worth a punt at 4H even if partner holds a lousy six-count. On that basis, a bid of 4D can be used to describe the diamond void and four-card heart support. East has spade control, a useful Q♣ and a fifth trump, making her worth a Roman Key-Card Blackwood bid. When West indicates two key-cards plus the trump queen, East knows these are A♣ and ♥AQ. If West also holds K♣, thirteen tricks look likely. 5NT asks West to name any king she has not yet shown (excluding the trump king) and West's 6C shows this card. East counts a spade, five hearts and at the very least four clubs tricks. On that conservative estimate, three diamonds would have to be trumped in dummy. But West is very likely to hold J♣ or a six-card suit, in which case six club tricks could make the hand easy – and so it is. An excellent grand slam bid on a combined 25pts – and J♠ and Q♦ are completely wasted.

Sadly, those holding the East-West cards did not play Super-Splinters and they only just made it to 6H.

To remember Super-Splinters (and you need to be sure that your partner understands the principle or you will suffer a high-level misunderstanding), these are the three key points:

1   A Reverse sequence is natural and forcing for one round.
2   A jump-rebid (when the normal rebid would have been a Reverse) is now a Splinter, showing a singleton, four-card support for partner's suit and values almost for game or better.
3   A double jump-rebid (when the normal rebid would have been a Reverse) is now a Super-Splinter, showing a void, four-card support for partner's suit, and values for game.

Slam-Going Manoeuvres

Grand Slam Force

I wrote about the Grand Slam Force in my first book (a long time ago) and, subsequently, with the ubiquity of Roman Key-Card Blackwood, I have wondered whether its time had passed. However, in the past few years, I have encountered numerous auctions where, having cue-bid, the one question a player still wants to ask is: how many of the top three trump honours do you hold? So I think that the GSF still has a place in our system and, on rare but exciting hands, you would be lost without it.

A bid of 5NT, when not proceeded by 4NT, asks partner how many of the top three honours in the agreed trump suit she holds.

> **6C = none**
> **6D = 1**
> **6H = 2**
> **7 of the agreed suit = 3**

These stepped responses are simple to remember and are more effective than the old-fashioned 'Josephine' responses of yesteryear.

West	East	West	East
♠ AK942	♠ Q853	1S	3S
♥ –	♥ 1072	4C	4D
♦ Q943	♦ AK82	4H	5D
♣ AKQJ	♣ 65	5NT	6D
		7S	

A simple example but one which illustrates cue-bidding and the GSF working together to result in a solid grand slam (barring North holding all four trumps).

Playing Jacoby-style Raises (see 123), East is maximum for a 3S raise but, when West starts to cue-bid, East will ensure that all her values are shown. East's second diamond cue-bid promises K♦ and *suggests* Q♦ also, but, here, having limited her hand and also holding Q♠, she is certainly justified in showing it. Those cards shown, West is worried only about a trump loser and so the GSF can be utilised. East's 6D response shows one of the top three spade honours and the grand slam can now be bid confidently.

Showing the trump queen you do not hold

The previous hand reminds me of the times when the trump queen can be shown in Roman Key-Card Blackwood – even when you do not hold it.

West	East	West	East
♠ A	♠ Q73	1H	3H
♥ AJ732	♥ K9854	4NT	5S
♦ KQJ64	♦ A82	**7H**	
♣ A3	♣ 65		

This deal occurred in the final of a big inter-club Teams-of-Four match. Partner and I were just playing a fairly simple Acol-based system, not including Jacoby-style Raises, so the 3H response showed 10–12pts with four-card heart support. When partner launched into RKCB, I decided that my fifth trump must surely represent the equivalent of the trump queen, since the auction marked partner with five hearts (with only a four-card heart suit, he – on this occasion it was a he – could scarcely have a hand strong enough to launch into Blackwood). So I bid 5S – two key-cards, plus the trump queen – and partner duly bid the grand slam, which made.

Since, at the other table, only 6H had been bid, there was something of a disagreement over my decision, with our opponents complaining to the powers-that-be. However, bridge is a game of judgement and decision-making, and of course you are allowed to take into account compensating factors when you are deciding what to bid.

So, if you know that you hold ten trumps between you, you are unlikely to require the trump queen and you can safely show it in your RKCB response. Don't be surprised if an opponent – or even partner – looks surprised.

Bidding 5 of a Major

There are many expert uses of strange jumps and raises to the five-level, several of which say to partner: pick a slam. I have always dreaded a partner doing this to me, since I'm not much good at picking a chocolate from a box, let alone knowing which slam to pick at the end of an inconclusive auction. Thankfully, the following suggestion involves asking partner questions about a specific element of her hand, for which there are unequivocal answers.

West	East	N	E	S	W
♠ AKJ854	♠ Q73				1S
♥ 3	♥ 84	2H	Dbl	4H	4S
♦ KQ4	♦ A982	NB	5S	NB	**6S**
♣ KJ3	♣ AQ76				

East's double over North's 2H overcall was a Negative-style Double, indicating interest in the minors, and 8/9pts or more. When West pushes on to 4S over South's barrage to 4H, East reckoned that West must hold a six-/seven-card spade suit, and values in the minors. Therefore, her hand is too good to pass. However, far more important than whether West holds ♠AK – which seems almost certain – is that East holds two quick heart losers. Her bid of 5S said: bid 6S if you have only one loser in hearts. This could be, most likely, a singleton, or ♥Kx. Here, with the singleton heart, West pushes on to the correct slam.

West	East	N	E	S	W
♠ AKJ8542	♠ Q73				1S
♥	♥ 842	2H	Dbl	4H	4S
♦ K74	♦ AQ82	NB	5S	NB	6H
♣ KJ3	♣ AQ7	NB	**7S**		

If we change the hand a little now, when East bids 5S, West must show that not only does she not have two losers in hearts, but she has first-round control in the suit. She does this by cue-bidding the suit, indicating A♥ or a void. Now, although it is a little frisky, East can probably risk 7S.

It is more risky since, if West did hold A♥, it is then far from certain that she would also hold both K♦ and K♣. Nonetheless, it seems to me to be a decent bet.

In a competitive auction, if you bid 5 of a major, it asks partner to bid 6 of the major with only one loser in the opponents' suit, or to cue-bid the opponents' suit if you hold the ace or void in that suit.

This jump can also be used when your opponents have not bid, and this time the question relates to the unbid suit.

West	East	West	East
♠ AK64	♠ QJ3	1H	2D
♥ AKQ87	♥ J53	2S	4H
♦ QJ	♦ AK972	**5H**	**NB**
♣ 53	♣ Q8		

	East	West	East
	♠ 852	1H	2D
	♥ J53	2S	4H
	♦ AK943	5H	**6H**
	♣ KQ		

Playing a simple Acol system with Lebensohl – a gadget described in *Control the Bidding* which provides extra description after a Reverse – the partner of a strong opener may be unable to show a little extra in trick-taking terms. Above, opposite both of East's hands, West reverses and East, stuck for a bid, jumps to game. West is probably worth one further try but, with two losers in clubs, she is a bit stuck for a constructive bid. Bidding 5H here asks East to bid 6H with second-round control in the unbid suit, or to cue-bid 6C if she holds A♣ or a void.

It could be argued that such sequences make finding the right lead easier for the opposition but, frankly, they are likely to be leading the unbid suit anyway and, if they suspect that dummy contains a long suit, they will be prepared to make just as aggressive leads as they will do now.

Ultimately, on the hands above, playing a simple system, this bid has found the right time to stop in 5H and the right time to be in 6H – and that seems pretty good.

In an uncontested auction, if you bid 5 of a major, it asks partner to bid 6 of the major with only one loser in the unbid suit, or to cue-bid the unbid suit if she holds the ace or void in that suit.

Special Overcalls and Continuations

Here are a couple of special overcalls that are worth having in your armoury and also some methods of competing further with special overcalls which I often see misused horribly.

Cue-bid over opponent's Weak Two opener

When an opponent opens a Weak Two bid, showing a weak hand with a six-card suit, a common pattern for another hand at the table is to have a strong hand with a six-card suit. When this suit is a major, this can be overcalled or even jump-overcalled. However, when your suit is a minor, 3NT may prove to be the best spot – and you do not want your opponents talking you out of the best game contract available.

West	N	E	S	W
♠ 43	–	–	2S	*3S*
♥ A5				
♦ AKQJ872				
♣ K96				

Simply to overcall 3D here would be to under-represent your hand considerably. If partner has a spade stop – and she may well – you want to be in 3NT. The correct bid here is to cue-bid your opponent's opening bid: 3S.

If partner holds a spade stop, anything from A♠ to ♠J10xx, she bids 3NT. If she holds no spade stopper, knowing that your bid is based on a long, solid minor suit, she bids 4C, and you pass or adjust to 4D. If partner is stronger, without a spade stopper, she can bid 5C, forcing you to pass or adjust to 5D.

These actions are similar to the responses to a Gambling 3NT opener.

So, the cue-bid over your opponent's Weak Two opener says that you have eight or nine tricks, based on a long minor suit, but lack any stopper in the opponent's suit.

Jump cue-bid over opponent's one opener

This is a rarer situation, since the one opener is stronger than the Weak Two opener, but it has cropped up half a dozen times just recently, so here it is. It's exactly the same as the cue-bid over a Weak Two, but here you jump, to distinguish this bid from whatever system of standard 'Parrot Bids' you might be playing (such as Michaels Cue-Bids, or Ghestem).

West	N	E	S	W
♠ A74	–	–	1H	*3H*
♥ 3				
♦ A53				
♣ AKQ643				

This is a superior approach to doubling and then bidding clubs, which would show a Strong Two opener-type hand, but would leave no space for investigating 3NT. Partner responds exactly as described above.

Further bidding after showing a two-suited hand

One of the key tenets of good bidding is that once you have shown your hand, there is no more to say. Yet players break this rule repeatedly and wonder why they end up in the wrong contract.

West	N	E	S	W
♠ Q3			1S	2NT
♥ 5	3S	NB	NB	?
♦ AK872				
♣ QJ987				

West must definitely pass now. Having made an Unusual NT overcall, showing 5-5 or longer in the two lowest-ranking unbid suits, East had a chance to bid over North's 3S and chose not to do so.

I recommend playing these two-suited overcalls as showing about 10pts upwards and, if you play something similar, then do not be seduced by your Q♠. That is useless to you if you play the contract, but may well be a defensive trick if you do not. You've made your bid, and that's the end of it.

West	N	E	S	W
♠ 3			1S	2NT
♥ 5	3S	NB	NB	?
♦ AK872				
♣ QJ9872				

This time, you have more shape than you have promised and, with your opponents stopping at the three-level, your partner could have the values to make 4C, 4D, or even game. Here, you can bid 4C, which shows 6-5 in your two suits (six clubs and five diamonds). If your suits are reversed – and you have greater length in the higher-ranking suit – you might try bidding 3NT, which should clearly still be for take-out. If your six-card suit is extra-good quality, you may simply decide to bid it.

West	N	E	S	W
♠ 3			1S	2NT
♥ A5	3S	NB	NB	?
♦ AK872				
♣ AJ987				

Here, Double is the correct bid. This states that you have no extra distribution, but you do have extra points which could be defensive. You do not want to leave your opponents in 3S undoubled. If your partner holds length in hearts and spades, she can pass and you are likely to defeat their contract. If she holds good-quality three-card support in one of your suits, she can bid on to 4C or 4D.

By the way, all this should be standard to you: extra distribution allows you to bid on; extra points allow you to double (but *not* to bid on). This is a consultative game and, if you are not prepared to involve your partner in most of your decisions, then take up Poker.

Exactly the same principles are in operation when partner bids and the opponents do not.

West	N	E	S	W
♠ 3			1S	2NT
♥ 5	NB	3C	NB	?
♦ AK8762				
♣ KJ987				

You are worth another bid here, since partner could have ♣Axx and A♥ and nothing else, and 5C would be a very decent contract. The correct bid is 3D. This shows 6-5 in diamonds and clubs, and allows you to get into the right contract when partner holds two- or three-card support for both your suits. It also indicates that your most likely shape is 6-5-1-1, and partner can now discount any likely value for K♥ or K♠ in her hand. (I hope that she has already dismissed queens or jacks in side suits as useless.)

West	N	E	S	W
♠ 8			1S	2NT
♥ A5	NB	3D	NB	?
♦ AKJ72				
♣ KQ986				

It would be tempting to jump to 5D here, but remember that partner could hold a doubleton in both your suits (or even a singleton in each!), so caution is advised. You've shown your shape, and partner has given simple preference only. Because of your extra values, you are worth one more try and, here, to bid 3S – your opponent's suit – would indicate a stronger hand than you have promised, but with no extra length. Now, if partner signs off now in 4D, it's time to give up.

Advanced Competitive Actions

At Duplicate Pairs, more than any other form of the game, aggressive and effective competition in the auction is essential to boosting your score. Within this strategy, lead-direction and level judgement must be sound. Probably the most important additional element to your system would be 'Fit jumps' and 'Fit non-jumps'.

Let's start with a quick revision of the basics, just to ensure that we are building on solid ground.

Support or shut up

When it comes to responding to an overcall, this is the default advice. If you dislike your partner's overcalled suit, even with quite a strong hand, it is better to pass, encouraging your opponents to re-enter the auction, than to argue with your partner.

The one exception to this basic rule would be converting a minor-suit overcall to a major suit, both for constructive reasons, with a view to the auction continuing, but also to adjust to a higher-scoring contract.

West	N	E	S	W
♠ KQJ97	1H	2C	NB	*2S*
♥ 975				
♦ K72				
♣ 86				

This is a perfectly acceptable change of suit since partner holds an opening hand and, if she has three-card support for you, game is still a possibility.

West	N	E	S	W
♠ 4	1H	1S	NB	*NB*
♥ Q952				
♦ AQ972				
♣ K86				

A clear-cut pass. Bidding 2D or 1NT ignores the key basic consideration: if the hand is a misfit, you want to be defending. Even with a sixth diamond, I would pass. Partner could have six spades herself and then you will play in 2S, with no guarantee that it will make. If you miss game once in 200 auctions, that is a price worth paying.

Simple support

The 'Total Trumps Principle' of raising partner to the same number of tricks as you have cards in your trump suit is sound, but should not be applied mindlessly.

West	N	E	S	W
♠ 973	1H	1S	NB	*NB*
♥ K852				
♦ J76				
♣ Q86				

This is a pass. It would be delightful to raise partner to 2S to inhibit the opener from bidding again, but the quality of your support and the shape of your hand should caution you against doing so.

Supporting partner's overcall following the TTP is pretty loose, but your hand should contain at least *one* of the following:

* a top trump honour;
* a singleton or void;
* two quick tricks (aces, king-queens) or better in outside suits.

If you hold none of these – as in the hand above – it is not a good idea. If you do bid on these hands, you will over-enthuse your partner, leave opponents with a better chance of penalising you when your trump suit breaks poorly, and encourage your partner to lead from holdings headed by ♠KJ, or even ♠AJ or ♠AQ – and you do not want that.

West	N	E	S	W
♠ K83	1H	2C	NB	*2S*
♥ 6				
♦ 98732				
♣ QJ107				

This six-count is ample, fulfilling two and a half out of three of the criteria: top spade honour, outside shortage, and tricks – if not quick ones – in clubs.

Unassuming Cue-Bids (UCB)

Any hand opposite an overcall with support for partner's suit with – opposite a one-level overcall – roughly, 11pts or more, or opposite a two-level overcall with 9/10pts or more, should first be indicated by a UCB. This is a bid of the opener's suit at the lowest available level.

West	N	E	S	W
♠ K73	1H	1S	NB	*2H*
♥ 95				
♦ A972				
♣ A862				

You have 11pts, all in aces and kings, three-card support or better for partner's suit, and a shortage in the opponent's hearts. If partner holds an opening hand, 4S is quite possible. This bid distinguishes a constructive game-possible hand from a mere barrage on poor values.

If partner is minimum, she rebids spades at the lowest available level. With hands approaching an opening hand or better, she can jump in her suit to indicate six cards, bid another suit to show 5-4, jump in another suit to show 5-5 or rebid NTs to indicate values in the opponent's suit.

Even if both opponents are bidding, the UCB can be used. So if, in the example above, South had raised to 2H, I would still want to bid 3H on the West hand.

A UCB promises three-card support or better for partner's suit, unless you have an especially strong hand and want to elicit more information about your partner's overcall.

West	N	E	S	W
♠ Q2	1H	1S	NB	*2H*
♥ 642				
♦ AK42				
♣ AK83				

The most likely contracts seem to be 4S or 3NT, but it is just possible that 5C or 5D might be right. Before making a decision, at least try to get a further description of your partner's hand. If she merely rebids 2S, you will be faced with a guess as to whether to bid 3S or 4S.

Hopefully, you will agree with the above actions and, if not, you and your partner at least agree what you would both do differently.

If you have already passed, then the point requirement for a UCB falls by a point or two: opposite a one-level overcall, a classy 9 or 10pts (made up of aces or kings in side suits, plus an honour or honours in partner's suit) is sufficient, and, opposite a two-level overcall, a very good 8/9pts would be the minimum for a UCB.

Fit non-jumps

The moment an opponent bids between your partner's overcall and your response, any bid you make guarantees support – or partial support – for your partner's suit. If you had a misfit with your partner you would stay out of the auction.

West	N	E	S	W
♠ J73	1H	1S	2C	2D
♥ 74				
♦ AKJ97				
♣ 862				

You have an eight-card fit or longer with partner in spades, so your opponents also have a fit in one of their suits and, soon, your side will almost certainly have to make a decision whether to play at the three-level or higher. By bidding diamonds here, you are imparting several key messages:

- I have a high-quality five-card diamond suit, headed by ace or king and another top honour. I would rather you led a diamond than a spade if we are defending.
- I have a doubleton honour or three small spades with you. If you return to spades, I will be perfectly content.
- I have a hand too weak to use a UCB, probably with a point range of 5–10pts.

When the auction continues like this, partner can judge what to do:

N	E	S	W		(a) East	(b) East
1H	1S	2C	2D		♠ KQ985	♠ AK842
3C	?				♥ A95	♥ Q65
					♦ Q86	♦ 52
					♣ 53	♣ Q53

With hand (a) East can bid on to 3D or 3S (West will probably convert 3D to 3S anyway) and that rates to make, whereas with hand (b) East will pass and leave 3C to play. This is right since 3C will probably fail, and neither 3D nor 3S can make.

Because partner has shown the diamond suit and spade support/good tolerance, East is able to judge whether to compete accurately based on knowing that on hand (a) she has a fit with partner's suit – meaning a double fit – or whether, as in hand (b) the second suit is mis-fitting with her hand. Hand (b) also contains more defensive values, such as Q♥ and Q♣.

If West had merely bid 2S initially, East would have no idea whether to pass or bid on.

This understanding leads us to playing this auction as a 'Fit non-jump' – simply meaning that, even without a jump in the auction, partner's bid is promising a (usually low quality) fit in partner's suit, with a high-quality suit of her own. These are non-forcing, competitive bids, which are extremely useful.

West's hand was hand (a), on which he bid 2D, but had it been hand such as (b), a simple raise to 2S would have been better.

(a) West	(b) West
♠ J73	♠ K76
♥ 74	♥ A4
♦ AKJ97	♦ J9743
♣ 862	♣ 862

Fit jumps

Fit jumps take this principle even further but allow for a combination of description and barrage based on distribution. When you have a trump fit, or a fit in two suits (a double fit), those are the times when you should compete to high levels. A double fit, especially, can lead to many tricks.

Points, apart from those concentrated in your suit(s), are largely irrelevant when it comes to judging levels in competitive auctions.

Again, to make a Fit jump is a weak manoeuvre, usually 5–10pts, but indicates both support for your partner's suit and good-quality length in a second suit. How high you bid will depend upon your trump fit and trick-taking potential and, again, not on points.

A jump to game in a new suit is to play – and is *not* a Fit jump.

Your Fit jump promises at least a five-card suit headed by ace or king and of good quality, plus a minimum of three-card support for partner's suit.

West	N	E	S	W
♠ 9873	1D	1S	2D	*3H*
♥ KQJ96				
♦ 97				
♣ 84				

West's bid of 3H indicates that she is happy to compete to the three-level, either in hearts or in spades. Since West is bidding at the three-level, this suggests four-card spade support (or a high-quality three-card support), as well as at least a five-card heart suit.

With more shape, and definitely four-card support for partner's suit, you can Fit jump to a higher level:

West	N	E	S	W
♠ J632	1C	1S	2C	*4D*
♥ 74				
♦ AK9762				
♣ 8				

With 6-4 in your two suits, raising to the four-level seems very reasonable. There is a case for just bidding 4S here, since it is more pre-emptive, but, if N/S have a double fit in hearts and clubs, your bid will help your partner to judge whether to bid on to 4S, 5S or even 6S later in the auction.

You can jump as high as you wish for a Fit jump, as long as it is not to game in the suit in which you jump. That bid is natural, to play, and would be weakish. It would not be agreeing partner's suit.

In the above examples, both opponents have been bidding, and your partner has overcalled, but a Fit jump or Fit non-jump can occur at any time in a competitive auction.

West	N	E	S	W
♠ 3	–	1H	2S	*4C*
♥ Q853				
♦ 75				
♣ AQ9874				

Whether South's jump-overcall is weak or intermediate strength, if you merely bid 4H and North then bids 4S, you will not know what to do, and partner will have no idea about your hand. To bid 4C as a Fit jump informs her that you are weak in terms of points but that you hold four-card heart support and probably six diamonds, where your values are concentrated.

In the recommended system, this bid cannot be confused with a Splinter since, once your opponents have bid, a Splinter should only be made in their suit, and not a new suit. Hence, this jump is clearly a shape-showing Fit jump which, ultimately, is a far more informative action.

N	E	S	W	(a) East	(b) East
-	1H	2S	4C	♠ 85	♠ 842
4S	?			♥ AJ974	♥ AJ642
				♦ AK4	♦ AK63
				♣ K53	♣ 5

On hand (a), East, with a fit in clubs and excellent controls, can bid on to 5C or 5H, which is very likely to make, whereas on hand (b), East, with a misfit in clubs, has great defensive potential and might well opt to double for penalties. Certainly East will not bid on.

You can also use Fit jumps after your opponent intervenes with a take-out double.

West	N	E	S	W
♠ 92	–	1H	Dbl	*3C*
♥ K84				
♦ 75				
♣ KQ9872				

You are extremely unlikely to be allowed to play in 2H, since the odds are very great that both your side and your opponents have an eight-card fit. First, your bid may dissuade North from showing his suit; second, your partner gains extra information and third, if partner passes your 3C bid, South may be reluctant to double again.

Although Fit jumps occur only when the auction is competitive, the principle can also be used in one auction when the opponents are not involved. This is nothing new – it used to be called a 'Jump-Shift After Passing' – which, I suppose, is technically what it is. However, it falls into the Fit jump category and can be very useful.

In this instance, the point range is 9–11pts and indicates a good pass with support for partner's suit, and a decent suit of your own. As a result of this fit, your hand is now worth opening values and hence you are indicating that, with a double fit, game will certainly be on. Additionally, if the auction subsequently becomes competitive – and these days it is quite likely to – then partner is better informed about your hand.

Having passed, partner opens 1D, and your opponents are silent.

(a) ♠ AQJ85	**(b)** ♠ KJ64	**(c)** ♠ J5
♥ 64	♥ 853	♥ KQJ87
♦ Q84	♦ AQ96	♦ QJ75
♣ 963	♣ 52	♣ 96

(a) You jump to 2S, indicating five decent spades and probably just three-card diamond support.

(b) 1S. To Fit jump, you must have a five-card suit. Simply show your major and plan to support diamonds later.

(c) 2H. Even with four-card diamond support, you can get in your five-card heart suit, and move towards a possible thin game contract.

With four-card support for partner's major suit, you should raise as usual, and not use a Fit jump.

Since you play Weak Two openers, having passed, your Fit jump will never show a six-card major, since you would have opened the hand at the one- or two-level. You may have a six-card minor, although this is rare.

Let's take a look at two examples of Fit jumps in action from some recent events.

```
Dealer East            ♠ 7
Game All               ♥ AJ104
                       ♦ Q9532
                       ♣ J107

  ♠ QJ94                              ♠ K86532
  ♥ 76            N                   ♥ 832
  ♦ 8         W       E               ♦ A
  ♣ A98652        S                   ♣ KQ4

                       ♠ A10
                       ♥ KQ95
                       ♦ KJ10764
                       ♣ 3
```

N	E	S	W
–	1S	2D	4C*
4D	4S	5D	NB
NB	5S		

West might have Splintered in South's overcalled suit, diamonds, but is probably a little too weak for such action. In any case, the 4C Fit jump described the hand more fully, strongly suggesting 6-4 shape in the black suits. When N/S competed effectively to 5D, East looked at her club support and realised that there was a big double fit, making it easy to continue to 5S.

Notice that, because there is a double-double fit – a double fit for both sides – N/S can make eleven tricks in hearts or diamonds, while

E/W are making ten tricks in either of their suits. Two down in 5S (South leading her singleton club and receiving a ruff later), undoubled, proved a fine result.

Dealer North
Love All

	♠ 5	
	♥ AQJ75	
	♦ KJ4	
	♣ K642	

	N	
W		E
	S	

♠ A1094
♥ 6
♦ 1086
♣ A10985

♠ KQJ83
♥ 10932
♦ 2
♣ QJ7

♠ 762
♥ K84
♦ AQ9753
♣ 3

N	E	S	W
1H	1S	3D*	4S
5H			

South's Fit jump to 3D turned out to be very useful. When West opted not to make a Fit non-jump to 4C (which would have indicated the type of hand he had) but instead raised to 4S – which was fine – North felt the double fit in the red suits warranted an extra trick, and he bid on. With only eight trumps, this would not normally be correct, but North knew that they had, at least, two eight-card fits, and probably an eight- and a nine-card fit. 5H duly made.

If West had bid 4C, I wonder whether East could have found the very difficult five-over-five sacrifice in 5S? This action is so rarely right but, knowing of a double-double fit, perhaps it could have been bid.

Remember that Fit non-jumps and Fit jumps are not a licence to withhold direct four-card support for partner's major suit, nor to overbid over your opponents' auctions. These bids are designed to help your side make as informed a decision as possible at high levels.

Doubling over opponents' pre-empts

The higher the standard of opponents you encounter, the more difficult they will be to play against. All you can do is to have in place some arrangements which ensure you have a decent chance of competing against such barrages.

A take-out double of a one-level opening bid traditionally promises all three of the remaining suits – either three- or four-card support. On very rare occasions, when you double and then bid a new suit, this shows a hand almost equivalent to a Strong Two opener, or a NT rebid shows an extra-strong balanced hand. The key understanding, however, is that a take-out double of a single suit at the one-level can never be a two-suited hand: it will almost always be all three suits and, rarely, a very strong single-suited hand.

Over a pre-emptive bid, however, your understanding should be different. To overcall a suit over a Weak Two opener, or a Weak Three opener, almost always shows a six-card suit with an opening hand. A jump-overcall must be played as strong (this is true even if you usually play weak or intermediate jump-overcalls), since you never make a weak bid over a weak bid, as this rarely makes sense.

Your RHO opens 2H (5–10pts). How should you compete with the following?

(a)	♠ AKJ85	(b)	♠ KJ8642	(c)	♠ AQJ984
	♥ 64		♥ 853		♥ 872
	♦ AQ4		♦ A6		♦ AKJ
	♣ 963		♣ A2		♣ 9

(a) 2S. Despite having only a five-card suit, you must stretch to bid at the two-level, since getting across your five-card major is important.

(b) 2S. This will show 10–14pts, or thereabouts, and usually a six-card suit.

(c) 3S. The jump-overcall over a weak bid by your opponent should indicate a strong hand: definitely a six-card suit, and around 16pts or more.

As you can show a strong single-suited hand with an overcall or jump-overcall, this frees up a take-out double to show either a three-suited hand, or a two-suited hand.

To double with a two-suited hand, you must be sure that you can handle any response your partner might make based on you having the more likely three-suited hand. To indicate a two-suited hand, if your partner bids the suit you do not possess, you then bid the cheaper of your two suits, allowing partner to pass or adjust, as she sees fit.

You will usually have 5-5 in your two suits to qualify as a two-suited hand but, if you are very strong, you may be forced to double with merely 5-4.

Your RHO opens 3D.

(d)	♠ AKJ8	**(e)**	♠ KQ864	**(f)**	♠ AK984
	♥ KQ74		♥ 53		♥ AKJ63
	♦ 4		♦ 6		♦ 32
	♣ Q963		♣ AKQ74		♣ 9

(d) The classic 4-4-4-1 take-out double.

(e) Double and, when partner inevitably bids 3H, or 4H, you then bid 3S/4S. This will show a two-suited hand with spades and clubs, and partner will adjust.

(f) Generally you would not play a Michael's Cue-bid or similar over a Weak Two opener, but you might bid 4D here to show 5-5 or longer in the two major suits. Failing that, double and, when partner bids 4C, you bid 4H and leave her to adjust. When she bids 5C – panic. Actually no, don't panic – bid 5H, and hope that she quietly passes or adjusts to 5S, 6H or 6S. If she bids 6C, hope for solid clubs and a singleton diamond, and it may well be the right contract.

If you are particularly strong, you may choose not simply to bid your cheapest suit at the lowest available level, but to jump to game.

Here is a deal that occurred in a big club Duplicate event. Few pairs reached the best contract.

Dealer North
E/W Game

	♠ 105	
	♥ AQJ10875	
	♦ 4	
	♣ J92	

♠ AKQ42			♠ 83
♥ 6	N		♥ 932
♦ AQ1096	W E		♦ KJ5
♣ 85	S		♣ AK743

	♠ J976	
	♥ K4	
	♦ 8732	
	♣ Q106	

N	E	S	W
3H	NB	NB	Dbl
NB	5C	NB	5D
NB	**6D**		

West doubled and East, quite correctly, jumped to 5C. When West corrected to 5D, showing a two-suited hand containing diamonds and spades, East decided that she held very good cards (West did not have values in hearts and could not hold more than ♦AQ so, surely, she had top spades), so she bid 6D – a fine contract even with the 4-1 trump break.

North led A♥ and another, forcing the hand with the long trumps to ruff and shorten her holding. West then played ♠AK and ruffed a low spade in dummy, before drawing all the remaining trumps. Now, West's spades are good and East's ♣AK take the eleventh and twelfth tricks.

Competing over opponents' artificial bids

There are many quite complex methods of competing over your opponents' artificial / conventional bids, but the simplest to operate is the one described here.

A double of an artificial bid is lead-directing

- At low levels, to double an opponent's artificial bid shows a five-card suit of good quality; one where you are happy for partner, if she holds support, to compete in that suit according to the Total Trumps Principle.

- If partner is on lead, this is definitely the suit you want her to play.
- A double of a Fourth Suit Forcing bid might show a four-card suit, and should not be supported by partner (the opponents are in a game-forcing situation having not yet found a fit).
- At higher levels, the double may show a void, and simply be lead-directional.
- None of these doubles promises values elsewhere in your hand.

Your LHO opens 1NT; partner passes. Your RHO bids 2D (Transfer). What should you bid, if anything, with the hands below?

(a)	♠ J85	(b)	♠ 6	(c)	♠ AQ72
	♥ 83		♥ 4		♥ 3
	♠ AQJ96		♦ KQJ87		♦ J7532
	♣ 972		♣ KQJ642		♣ AJ6

(a) Double. Lead-directing, promising a high-quality five-card suit.

(b) Double. Lead-directing, showing five diamonds or more. If your opponents bid to 4H, you will probably bid 5C next. Partner should be aware that you are likely to be 6-5 in your two suits, not necessarily with longer diamonds.

(c) Pass. Your diamonds are not nearly high enough quality and, if your opponents stop in 2H, you will want to double on the next round for take-out.

- A double of an Acol-style 2C bid would show five decent clubs, and a double of an Acol-based strong but unspecified-suit 2D opening bid would show diamonds.
- A double of Stayman shows clubs; a double of a negative response to Stayman of 2D would show diamonds, and so on.
- If, instead of doubling a conventional bid, you bid that suit, you are showing a high-quality six-card suit with some outside values.

Your LHO opens 1NT (12–14); partner passes. Your RHO bids 2C (Stayman).

(d) ♠ 764　　　**(e)** ♠ KQ52　　　**(f)** ♠ QJ98
♥ 83　　　　　　♥ 6　　　　　　　♥ 3
♠ J96　　　　　♦ 87　　　　　　♦ 532
♣ AKJ85　　　♣ AQJ842　　　♣ AQJ62

(d) Double, showing a good-quality five-card club suit.
(e) 3C, showing a six-card club suit. If your opponents alight in 4H, at favourable vulnerability you might bid 4S next.
(f) Double, showing a good-quality five-card club suit. If your opponents stop in 2H, you will bid 2S next.

After a conventional bid by your opponents, you often have an efficient way of showing a two-suited hand by first doubling the conventional bid to show that you hold that suit, and then bidding your other suit later. Before deciding how best to describe your hand, always ask yourself how you expect the auction to run and then arrange your bids in the most economical, space-efficient manner possible.

Bidding the suit your opponent is actually showing is a strong take-out manoeuvre

The most frequent occasion this action might be taken is after your opponents make a Transfer bid.

Your LHO opens 1NT (12–14); partner passes. Your RHO bids 2D (Transfer).

(a) ♠ AJ64　　　**(b)** ♠ KQ52　　　**(c)** ♠ 8
♥ K83　　　　　♥ 6　　　　　　　♥ KJ63
♠ 62　　　　　　♦ QJ87　　　　　♦ AQJ5
♣ KJ85　　　　♣ AKJ4　　　　　♣ Q742

(a) Pass. To double now would show good diamonds, and you have no five-card suit to bid. If your opponents subside in 2H, you can double for take-out subsequently to compete the part-score.
(b) 2H. By bidding the suit your opponent has *shown,* you are making

a strong take-out of, here, hearts. This bid would normally show 15pts or more, with a well-shaped take-out hand.

(c) Pass. Unsuitable for any action, probably at any time in this auction.

Generally, after a Transfer, if you have a hand suitable for a take-out double of the suit your opponent is *showing*:

> **With 7–10pts, you will wait for the Transfer to play out and, if they stop at the two-level, you may compete.**
>
> **With 11–14pts, you will probably compete at your second turn once the Transfer suit has been named.**
>
> **With 15pts or more, you can bid the suit your opponents are showing to indicate a strong take-out of their suit immediately.**

This principle can be applied to other situations also. For example, your partner opens 1NT (12–14); your RHO bids 2D (Asptro, showing spades and another suit, 5-4 distribution either way around).

(d) ♠ 54	**(e)** ♠ 92	**(f)** ♠ 8
♥ KQ83	♥ KQJ6	♥ KJ63
♦ A53	♦ AQJ87	♦ QJ95
♣ KJ42	♣ J4	♣ QJ42

(d) 2S. A take-out of spades – the suit your opponent has *shown*. Your side has game on, you just have to find the correct denomination. If your partner has one good stopper or better in spades, she will bid 2NT or 3NT depending on strength, otherwise she will seek a 4-4 major-suit fit, or a 4-4 / 5-3 minor-suit fit.

(e) 2S. Again, game is almost certainly on. If partner bids 3C, you will have to bid 3D. This should show diamonds and hearts.

(f) 2S. Risky, but probably worth bidding now since, if you pass and your opponents bid to 3S, you will be faced with a tough choice. If partner holds decent spades and rebids 3NT, at least she will know where most of the remaining points are located.

When an artificial bid is used which defines only one suit, a bid of that suit is for take-out, usually showing values sufficient to reach game by your side.

Remain aware that with one solid stopper or better in the opponent's shown suit, partner will rebid NTs, with a minimum hand at the lowest available level; with a maximum hand, she will bid to 3NT.

Competing after opponents use the Unusual NT overcall

The main use of the Unusual NT overcall should be to consult partner about a possible sacrifice. Most players use a point count ranging from a well-structured 10pts (points in the long suits, good intermediate cards) to a very strong hand. Over such pre-emptive intervention, it is important to distinguish between different types of hand, whether or not your side has a fit, and to provide partner with a decent idea of your strength.

Below is a standard type of defence to the Unusual No-trump overcall, although there are many subtle variations.

Assuming that partner opens 1H or 1S, and your RHO overcalls 2NT, these are the various responses available:

Pass: Indicates a weak hand with limited tolerance for partner's suit, or a stronger hand with shortage in partner's suit (and also probably the other major suit).

If you pass, followed by making a double of your opponents' bid, this is for penalties.

Double: Suggests 10pts or more, with two-card support or fewer for partner's major suit, a balanced-ish hand with an emphasis on the minors. If agreed, may show four cards in the other major (as in Negative-style Doubles). Partner is likely to pass that double for penalties with a balanced hand, but with 5-5 in the majors, or a six-card major suit, is likely to bid on, with knowledge that you hold values.

Three of partner's major: Shows four-card support for partner's suit with 5–9pts.

Three of other major: Shows six-card suit (possibly very high-quality five-card suit), forcing.

3C: This bid shows 10pts / eight losers, or stronger with good three-card or four-card support for partner's major suit. Partner may rebid her suit at the three-level to show a minimum, jump to the four-level in her major suit or, with 15pts or more, and with only a four-card major suit, she can rebid 3NT.

If you hold four-card support with ruffing values, you may then convert 3NT to four of partner's major.

3D: This shows an intermediate-range hand of 8–11pts, with high-quality five- or six-card suit in the other major, promising two- or three-card support for partner's major suit. With a singleton or void in partner's suit, the hand is too likely to be a misfit for you to want to introduce a new suit at the three-level.

Four of partner's major: At least four-card support for partner's suit with game-going values.

Four of other major: Game-going values with a high-quality six- or seven-card suit. To play.

Partner opens 1S; RHO overcalls 2NT (Unusual NT overcall).

(a)	♠ AJ64	(b)	♠ KQ52	(c)	♠ 8
	♥ Q7832		♥ K742		♥ AK63
	♠ 962		♦ Q87		♦ Q985
	♣ 5		♣ J4		♣ J982

(a) 3S. A weak competitive raise.
(b) 3C. A strong (10–12pts) invitational raise with three-card support or more.
(c) Double. You dislike partner's suit and, at the moment, the hand seems to be a misfit. For this reason, defence seems the best option.

(d)	♠ KQ7	(e)	♠ Q2	(f)	♠ 832
	♥ AJ432		♥ KQJ986		♥ AKQJ9
	♠ 53		♦ A7		♦ 95
	♣ J42		♣ 742		♣ 942

(d) 3C. Showing good three-card support or four-card spade support, with 10pts or more. Partner can rebid 3S to show a minimum hand, 4S for a stronger hand; 3NT shows 15pts or more with a balanced hand and stoppers in both minors.

(e) 3H. Natural and forcing.

(f) 3D. Shows a high-quality five-card or six-card suit in other major, plus tolerance for partner's suit; not strong enough to force to game but decent to compete. Usually 8–11pts.

When an opponent intervenes with a two-suited hand, this increases the likelihood that partner started with a five-card suit or longer, but be aware that the Unusual NT overcall – indeed, any two-suited overcall – tips you off to likely poor breaks in the side suits, so do not stretch to bid a contract with only an eight-card fit.

If you end up playing the contract, you have been given a distributional blueprint by the overcaller, which must be kept in mind while planning and playing the hand.

'Moysian' Fits

A Moysian fit, named after Alphonse Moyse Jr, refers to a 4-3 trump fit – a contract which often presents problems. Two-thirds of the time, one opponent will have four trumps and, hence, the drawing of trumps may be problematic.

In the bidding, you largely want to consider in which hand you are most likely to be made to trump. If it is the hand containing the long trump holding, unless useful loser-on-loser plays can be found, you will be forced out of control. Therefore, when considering a 4-3 trump fit, ask yourself: will I be able to trump my weak suit in the hand with the shorter (three-card) trump holding? If so, the 4-3 fit may well succeed.

Other considerations that might influence your decision should include the quality of your seven-card trump fit, especially those in the hand with four trumps, and whether or not you hold the trump ace and, ideally, the trump king also. Drawing trumps with only seven becomes far more troublesome when you are missing the control cards.

Dealer North
Love All

		♠ 3	
		♥ KQ2	
		♦ AJ653	
		♣ KJ54	

♠ KQJ6		♠ 109742
♥ 8654	N	♥ 73
♦ 97	W E	♦ Q108
♣ 982	S	♣ AQ10

♠ A85	
♥ AJ109	
♦ K42	
♣ 763	

N	E	S	W
1D	NB	1H	NB
2C	NB	2S*	NB
3H	NB	**4H**	

South's 2S is Fourth Suit Forcing, and North shows her three-card heart support now. Knowing North's 1-3-5-4 shape, South should realise that a single spade stop is unlikely to be sufficient for 3NT and should opt for the Moysian fit.

South has good trumps, the trump ace, and the perfect spade holding opposite a known singleton.

West may lead K♠, but should probably start with a trump. Whichever lead is made, declarer does best to take a diamond finesse leading low from hand to J♦ in dummy. Since West did not lead a diamond, it is unlikely that she holds a singleton. If East has one, E/W will not be able to cash two club tricks and make a diamond ruff. As the cards lie, four diamond tricks are assured, plus four trumps and A♠, so South must ensure a spade ruff before drawing all the trumps.

When Weak Jump-Overcalls are Not Weak

If you don't play weak jump-overcalls, but instead intermediate-strength jump-overcalls, then this section is still for you because, in certain positions, your jump-overcalls are not their usual strength.

Protective position

In the standard fourth-seat protective position, most bids could be quite weak: one-level overcalls could be 6pts or more; two-level overcalls 8/9pts or more; doubles 9pts or more, 1NT probably 11–14pts.

It makes sense, therefore, to have some bids which are definitely strong. In this way, when you have a genuinely strong hand opposite a partner's weak hand, you can still reach game safely.

For these reasons, jump bids in the fourth-seat protective position are played as strong.

In this protective position, a jump-overcall of a suit should show a six-card suit, with seven to eight playing tricks, or around 14pts upwards.

A 2NT overcall is not an Unusual NT overcall, but is instead a strong balanced hand, promising at least one stopper in the opponent's suit, indicating 18–21pts (slightly fewer if you hold a five- or six-card minor suit).

Your LHO opens 1H. Partner and RHO both pass.

(a)	♠ K85	(b)	♠ AKQ852	(c)	♠ AJ6
	♥ 83		♥ 96		♥ QJ102
	♦ 543		♦ AJ8		♦ KJ5
	♣ AJ985		♣ K4		♣ AK4

(a) 2C is a quite acceptable overcall here in the protective position. This is at least an ace short of the usual values required for a two-level overcall. If you would have bid it in any position – please *don't*!

(b) 2S. The jump-overcall here is strong, indicating 14pts or more; seven to eight playing tricks, with a high-quality six-card suit.

(c) 2NT. Balanced-ish, 18–21pts, at least one stopper in the opponent's suit. Stayman and Transfers are available to partner if your LHO now passes.

(d) ♠ 10964	**(e)** ♠ AKJ8643	**(f)** ♠ 8
♥ QJ7	♥ 54	♥ KJ63
♠ AJ9	♦ AK6	♦ QJ95
♣ K108	♣ 4	♣ Q942

(d) 1NT. In the protective position, this shows 11–14pts, with one stopper or more in the opponent's suit. At Duplicate Pairs, some experts bid this without a stopper. At Teams-of-Four, Chicago or Rubber Bridge, you might simply choose to pass, but at Duplicate, the odds favour you bidding.

(e) Double. You could punt 4S, but your plan is to double first and then jump to 3S over whatever your partner responds (unless, amazingly, they show some values, when, obviously, you can bid 4S directly). In this way, if partner has three jacks, you can stay out of a hopeless game but, if partner has an ace, or a KQ, she can bid 4S scientifically. This auction shows a hand stronger than a jump-overcall, indicating close to nine playing tricks or better.

(f) Double. Just to illustrate how weak the protective position can be – and how wide a range a double is – this is, of course, a take-double.

Pre-protective position

It almost sounds unbelievable, but if you've embraced 'Fit non-jumps', then this type of title won't phase you. Simply, this is a position when your opponents quickly agree a suit weakly, usually with a simple raise, and you have a hand where you feel that, if you pass, and the opener now passes, your partner may struggle to protect.

Put another way: once your opponents agree a suit, your bids are largely made on shape, with little reference to your point count.

Your LHO opens 1H, partner passes, and RHO bids 2H. What would you bid?

(a)	♠ K852	**(b)**	♠ QJ743	**(c)**	♠ J96
	♥ 8		♥ 96		♥ 982
	♠ QJ93		♦ A82		♦ AK5
	♣ KJ85		♣ 532		♣ AJ42

(a) Double. You should bid here because, if your partner has passed on a flat 12 count, she will not be able to bid if the opener passes 2H. You have the shape: she does not (she is very likely to hold three or four hearts). If your opponents bid on to game, you have provided a little information but, for an intelligent declarer, not much that she couldn't work out for herself.

(b) 2S. Again, because you are short in hearts, your partner may well hold three of them, making it difficult for her to find a bid if 2H is passed out. So, you bid.

(c) Pass. Here, you have no shape, you hold three hearts, so your partner is likely to be short. If your opponents pass out 2H, your partner should be able to dredge up a shape-describing bid.

(d)	♠ AQJ985	**(e)**	♠ Q852	**(f)**	♠ QJ6
	♥ 83		♥ A109		♥ 7
	♠ AQJ		♦ AJ8		♦ AK4
	♣ 75		♣ AKJ		♣ AKQJ86

(d) 3S. The jump-overcall here is now strong, showing 14pts or more, high-quality six-card suit, seven to eight playing tricks.

(e) Double. This is not the protective position, so 2NT is not natural – it would be the Unusual NT overcall. You must double and then rebid no-trumps over partner's response. If your opponents continue to 3H, you should double again – partner will hold a five-card suit 99 per cent of the time and, if she doesn't, she can pass your second double for penalties (not wishing to bid at the four-level with possibly only seven or eight trumps between you).

(f) 3H. As discussed earlier, this bid states that you can make 3NT, but you lack any stopper in the opponents' suit. It is based on a long, solid minor suit so, if partner cannot bid 3NT, she must convert to 4C, which, here, you would pass. This is superior to playing this bid as a Michael's Cue-bid or similar.

The Bidding System – The Convention Card

Over the years, my advanced students have learnt many of the gadgets and conventions that I have recommended and these have been formed into a powerful Acol-based system. The system has been contributed to by international players, and it is the basis of what I play myself. It has been found to work, bringing national and county titles, and many a club Duplicate, all over the world. Here are the basic details:

Basic System: Acol-style with weak twos in major suits

1NT = 12–14pts; may **not** contain five-card major

Responses
2C = Stayman
2D = Transfer to hearts
2H = Transfer to spades
2S = Good-quality six-card minor with 9/10pts, or slam-going minor two-suiter
2NT = 11/12pts

Action after opponents double 1NT: natural
Opener may re-double to show a five-card minor

OPENING BIDS
1NT is 12–14 HCP; in the fourth seat: 11–14pts
Responses: Stayman, Transfers

All one-level opening bids are four cards or longer; 10–20pts
Responses: limit raises based on LTC; Jacoby-Style non-game-forcing 2NT raise; Splinters

2H and 2S – weak: 5–9pts; third-in-hand 3–11pts
Responses: 2NT = game enquiry; change of suit non-forcing

2D: strong one- or three-suited hand; eight to nine playing tricks; or 4-4-4-1, 19pts +
Responses: 2H = relay – 2NT rebid = 4-4-4-1 shape; suits natural, non-forcing

2C: game-forcing: nine playing tricks or more, distributional; 23pts + balanced
Responses: 2H = no ace, king or multiple queens; 2D = one of the aforementioned; any other bid = positive = five-card suit or longer, two out of the three top honours; 2NT = positive heart response

2NT: good 20–22pts; may contain five- or six-card minor; five-card major suit; singleton ace
Responses: five-card major Stayman; 3D, 3H, 3S Transfers
3S Transfer shows 5-4 or longer in minor suits

3 bids: weak 5–9pts; seven-card suit; third-in-hand may be six-card suit
4 bids: weak 9–13pts; seven-card suit or longer

DEFENSIVE METHODS AFTER OPPONENTS OPEN
Simple overcall: five cards or longer
Responses: pre-emptive raises, UCB, Fit jumps, Fit non-Jumps

Jump-overcall: weak, 3–9pts, six-card suit; protective: strong

Cue-bid: Michaels Cue-bid; might be 5-4 in fourth seat

1NT in direct position: 16–18pts; Protective: 11–14pts
Responses: Stayman, Transfers
2NT in direct position: Unusual NT; Protective 18–21pts

CONVENTIONAL DEFENCES

Opponents open:	Defence:
Weak 1NT	Asptro
Strong 1NT	Asptro
Weak Two	Double = Take-Out (T.O.); 2NT = 17–20
Weak Three	Double = T.O.

4-bids	Double = T.O.
Multi 2♦	Simple "Dixon"*
Strong 1♣	C.R.O.S.H.*

* rarely used; to be researched if required.

SLAM CONVENTIONS
Roman Key-Card Blackwood:
    5C = 0 or 3
    5D = 1 or 4
    5H = 2 without trump queen
    5S = 2 with trump queen
    5NT asks partner to name king
    2 kings: bid 6NT
Cue-Bidding; Exclusion Blackwood
Grand Slam Force: 5NT asks for top three trump honours:
    5C = 0
    5D = 1
    5H = 2
    Seven of agreed suit = 3

COMPETITIVE AUCTIONS
Negative doubles apply to all levels; promise other major to 2NT
1C–1D–Dbl = four spades and four hearts
Cue-bid of opponent's overcall: game-forcing
Fit jumps

After opponents double for take-out:
Re-double = 10pts +
New suit: natural
Jump in new suit: Fit jump
Jump raise: weak; four-card support
2NT: 10pts+ four-card support
Double of artificial bid: natural / lead-directional
Bid of suit shown by artificial bid: take-out
Double of natural bid: take-out / penalties

Stayman, Transfers, Five-card major Stayman (opposite 2NT),
UCB, Splinters, Advance Cue-Bids, UNT, Michael's Cue-bids,
Jacoby-Style 2NT Raises

Opening Leads

Standard system:
> fourth highest
> top-of-sequence
> top-of-rubbish

Against suits	AK	AKx*	KQ10	KQx	KJ10	K109	QJ10	AKxx*
	QJx	J10x	10xx	109x	987x	10xxx	Hxx	
	Hxxx	Hxxxx	xx	Xxx*	xxxx			
Against NTs	AKx	AKxx*	AJ10x	KQ10	KQx	KJ10	K109	QJ10
	QJx	J10x	10xx	109x	987x	10xxx	Hxx	
	Hxxx	Hxxxx	xx	Xxx*	xxxx			

H = honour card, jack or higher; x = intermediate, nine or lower
* Choice of card dependent upon situation or signal desired

CARDING METHODS
Signals: against Suits *and* NT contracts
On partner's lead: if ace led = attitude; ace played second-in-hand = attitude; otherwise = count
On opponent's lead: count

Discards: against Suits *and* NT contracts
Suit-preference / occasionally, count

Signal: High = encouraging; Low = discouraging
Count: High = even number of cards; Low = odd number of cards

Other Reading

In this book, I refer to some of my previous books which outline the basic elements of the bidding system and card play:

For the bidding: *Control the Bidding*
For card play: *Winning Ways to Play Your Cards*
For Duplicate bridge: *Mendelson's Guide to Duplicate Bridge*

Acknowledgements

Many thanks to Duncan Proudfoot, who gamely commissions my bridge books without being told with clarity what the next one might contain, trusting me to try to make them informative and entertaining. Much gratitude to Rebecca Sheppard for co-ordinating the production and to Nick Fawcett for interpreting my manuscript and cajoling me into making it intelligible. Thanks also to Rita Gallinari, and to my many loyal students whose enthusiasm inspires these tomes.

However seriously you take your game, please remember to enjoy yourselves. Sometimes, strangely – and sadly – that concept gets lost...

Paul Mendelson
London